THE ULTIMATE GUIDE TO
WEDDING MUSIC

BY ELIZABETH & ALEX LLUCH

Professional Wedding Consultants and
Authors of Nineteen Bestselling Wedding Books

THE ULTIMATE GUIDE TO WEDDING MUSIC
Published by Wedding Solutions Publishing, Inc.

Copyright © 2002, 2005

Musical recordings used under license from Naxos of America, Inc., 416 Mary Lindsay Polk Drive, Suite 509, Franklin, TN 37067, www.naxosusa.com. All recordings and this compilation © 2000 HNH International Ltd. All rights reserved. Unlawful duplication is a violation of applicable laws.

Front Cover Photographs Provided By:
Left: www.Comstock.com
Center: Arts & Culture; Photodisc Collection/Getty Images
Right: Karen French
Karen French Photography
8351 Elmcrest, Huntington Beach, CA 92646
Telephone: 714.968.5839
E-mail: info@karenfrenchphotography.com
www.karenfrenchphotography.com

Special Thanks to:
Rebecca Davis, Naxos of America
Manager of Publicity and Promotions
and Wedding Music Consultant

Printed in China

ISBN:1-887169-45-8

THE WEDDING OF

_____

&

_____

WHO WILL BE MARRIED ON

_____

AT

_____

DEDICATED TO...

All Brides and Grooms. May the rest of your lives be filled

with Music, Laughter, and Love.

CONTENTS

• INTRODUCTION 7

• THE COMPANION MUSIC CD 9

• CEREMONY MUSIC 15

   PRELUDE...15

   PRE-PROCESSIONAL 17

   PROCESSIONAL AND BRIDE'S ENTRANCE 18

   CEREMONY AND UNITY CANDLE 20

   RECESSIONAL 21

   INTERLUDE/POSTLUDE 22

• RECEPTION MUSIC 23

   COCKTAIL HOUR 23

   NEWLYWEDS' ENTRANCE 23

   DINNER 24

   FIRST DANCE...24

   FAMILY DANCES 29

   TOASTS 32

   BOUQUET TOSS 33

   GARTER REMOVAL AND TOSS...34

CONTENTS

CAKE CUTTING 36

MONEY DANCE 38

ETHNIC DANCES 40

LAST DANCE 42

GENERAL 44

• MUSIC OPTIONS 47

• HIRING A MUSIC PROFESSIONAL 51

• COMPARISON CHART FOR HIRING A MUSIC PROFESSIONAL 57

• SIGNING THE CONTRACT 63

• WEDDING MUSIC TIMELINE 65

• CREATING YOUR MUSIC STYLE 67

• WRITING A MUSIC PROGRAM 77

MUSIC PROGRAM - CEREMONY 78

MUSIC PROGRAM - RECEPTION 80

• MUSIC CHECKLISTS 85

EQUIPMENT CHECKLIST 86

THINGS TO DO CHECKLIST 86

• A CRASH COURSE IN CLASSICAL MUSIC 87

• LYRICS FOR 100 POPULAR WEDDING SONGS 91

INTRODUCTION

Congratulations on your engagement! You are about to start planning the happiest day of your life. Planning your wedding can be fun and exciting, but it can also be very stressful. Wedding Solutions Publishing, Inc. has helped over a half a million brides plan the wedding of their dreams through our 19 best-selling wedding planners. Now we can offer you even more help with *The Ultimate Guide to Wedding Music*.

You want your wedding to be beautiful and memorable. Music plays a big part in making that happen. It will serve as the soundtrack to your day and will help convey the feelings you have for each other and for your families and friends. So how do you find the perfect music and how do you hire the best people to perform the pieces you have chosen? *The Ultimate Guide to Wedding Music* will help you find the right music for your entire wedding, from the ceremony to the reception, and give you useful advice on locating, interviewing and hiring musicians and DJs.

Also enclosed in this book is a full-length classical music CD containing excerpts from 99 classical pieces. Each piece is performed by world-class musicians, and is of the highest quality recording. Use this CD to familiarize yourself with music that can be performed during various parts of your wedding.

This book outlines the main parts of the wedding, the ceremony and reception, from a musical perspective. The ceremony and reception are categorized into different time-frames or events where specific music should be played. In addition to a description of each time-frame, this book also provides suggestions of what type of music is typically played, as well as a list of song options, complete with the title, artist, album and genre.

Since it is often difficult to finalize your music choices, we have also provided lyrics to 100 of the most popular songs for weddings. Weddings are so special that sometimes the words alone encourage you to choose one song over another. We hope the lyrics provided give you options and ideas or help you make your final decisions.

INTRODUCTION

To make choosing music and hiring the right people as easy as possible, we have also included worksheets and comparison charts. These worksheets can be used to narrow down your search for the perfect song and to compare musicians and DJs. You will also be able to create a music program for the ceremony and reception, noting what music should be played and when. These worksheets are found throughout the book and can be photocopied if you need more.

We hope you will find *The Ultimate Guide to Wedding Music* a valuable resource, one that will help to make planning the wedding of your dreams as stress-free as possible!

Sincerely,

Elizabeth H. Lluch

THE COMPANION MUSIC CD

WEDDING SOLUTIONS PUBLISHING, INC. IS VERY PLEASED to have partnered with Naxos, a highly respected classical music recording company, to bring you a very unique companion CD. This compact disc contains excerpts from 99 of the most popular classical music pieces for weddings. It is intended to simplify the task of choosing the right music for your ceremony and reception.

Put the CD in your stereo and listen to the selections with your fiancé and/or family members. Have a pen and paper handy to make notes as you listen. Write down the track numbers of the pieces you like and compare notes after you have finished listening to the CD. Within the section, you will find the track listing for the Companion CD along with the corresponding Naxos catalog number for easy reference. Once you have chosen the perfect piece for each part of your ceremony and reception, stop into any music retailer to purchase the CD with the full-length piece. Having the Naxos catalog number handy will allow you to easily locate the album you desire.

TRACK LISTING FOR COMPANION CD

PROCESSIONAL...

1. Wagner, Bridal Chorus (from Lohengrin) 8.550790

2. Pachelbel, Canon in D 8.550790

3. Vivaldi, Guitar Concerto in D Major, Largo 8.550274

4. Vivaldi, Winter, Largo (from The Four Seasons) 8.550056

5. Clarke, Trumpet Voluntary 8.550790

6. Gabrieli, Canzon V 8.553873

7. Handel, Overture (from Royal Fireworks Music) 8.550109

8. Handel, Air (from Water Music) 8.550109

9. Handel, See the Conqu'ring Hero 8.556665

10. Handel, Larghetto (from Xerxes) 8.550521

11. Handel, Oboe Concerto, Adagio 8.550102

12. Monteverdi, Toccata (from L'Orfeo) 8.554094-95

13. Charpentier, Te Deum 8.550581

14. Mendelssohn, Sonata for Organ, Op. 65, No. 3 ....8.553583

15. Purcell, Trumpet Tune 8.550790

16. Telemann, Trumpet Concerto in D, Allegro 8.553531

17. Mussorgsky, Promenade (from Pictures at an Exhibition) 8.553249

18. MacDowell, To A Wild Rose 8.559010

19. Beethoven, Pathétique Sonata..8.550045

20. Satie, Gymnopedie No. 1 ....8.554166

TRACK LISTING FOR COMPANION CD

RECESSIONAL...

21. Mendelssohn, Wedding March 8.550790

22. Bach, Fugue in E-Flat Major (from St. Anne) 8.550184

23. Walton, Crown Imperial 8.553981

24. Vivaldi, Spring, Allegro (from The Four Seasons) 8.555319-20

25. Vivaldi, Concerto for two Trumpets in B, Allegro 8.550014

26. Handel, Hallelujah Chorus (from The Messiah) 8.550779

27. Handel, Arrival of the Queen of Sheba 8.556665

28. Handel, Hornpipe (from Water Music) 8.550109

29. Handel, Hornpipe (from Concerto Grosso Op 6, No 7) 8.550102

30. Beethoven, Ode to Joy 8.556623

31. Telemann, Trumpet Concerto in D II, Allegro 8.553531

32. Telemann, Trumpet Concerto in B, Allegro 8.550104

33. Widor, Toccata 8.550790

34. Bach, Brandenburg Concerto No. 4, Allegro 8.554608

35. Bach, Badinerie 8.550014

36. Bach, Cantata No. 51 ....8.550643

37. Dubois, Toccata (from Douze Pieces) 8.550955

38. Haydn, String Quartet D-Major Op.64, No.5, Hob.III 8.554429

39. Haydn, String Quartet F-Major Op.50, No.5, Hob.III....................8.553984

40. Schumann, Piano Quintet in E Flat-Major Op.44 ....8.554429

TRACK LISTING FOR COMPANION CD

PRELUDE/INTERLUDE/POSTLUDE/INCIDENTAL...

41. Albinoni, Adagio "Giazotto" 8.550790

42. Bach, In Dulci Jubilo 8.550102

43. Bach, Jesu, Joy of Man's Desiring (from BWV 147) 8.556656

44. Bach, Sheep May Safely Graze (from BWV 208) 8.550790

45. Bach, Air on a G String 8.556656

46. Bach, Sonata No.2 in E flat-major, Siciliano 8.554166

47. Boellmann, Toccata (from Suite Gothique Op.25) 8.550790

48. Vaughan-Williams, Hymn Prelude on Rhosymedre 8.550582

49. Vierne, Carillon de Westminster..8.550955

50. Gounod, Ave Maria 8.550790

51. Schubert, Ave Maria (for Voice)...8.553751

52. Handel, Ombra mai fu (from the Opera Xerxes).......................8.550790

53. Handel, Let the Bright Seraphim 8.553735

54. Handel, Pastoral Symphony..8.556665

55. Puccini, Musetta's Waltz (from La Boheme).............................8.553151

56. Schubert, Ave Maria (for Organ) 8.550790

57. Mozart, Alleluia (from Exsultate Jubilate) 8.550495

58. Grieg, I Love You 8.553781

59. Schubert, Du Bist die Ruhe (You are My joy) 8.550476

60. Franck, Panis Angelicus (O Lord Most Holy) 8.553751

TRACK LISTING FOR COMPANION CD

PRELUDE/INTERLUDE/POSTLUDE/INCIDENTAL-CONT'D...

61. Gluck, Dance of the Blessed Spirits 8.554166

62. Faure, Sicillienne Op. 78 ....8.554166

63. Faure, Aprés un Rêve 8.550791

64. Elgar, Chanson de Matin 8.554166

65. Debussy, Arabesque 8.554166

66. Bizet, Intermezzo from Carmen 8.554166

67. Elgar, Salut d'amour 8.554166

68. Grieg, Morning from Peer Gynt 8.554166

69. Debussy, Prélude à l'après midi d'un faun 8.554166

70. Boccherini, String Quintet Op. 13, Minuet 8.550731

71. Greensleeves, Traditional (arr. by Buck) 8.550141

72. Saint-Saëns, The Swan (from Carnival of the Animals) 8.550791

73. Massenet, Meditation (from Thaïs) 8.550306

74. Mendelssohn, On Wings of Song 8.550646

75. Mozart, Piano Concerto No. 21, Andante 8.550202

76. Torelli, Trumpet Concerto, 2nd Movement 8.550102

77. Mozart, Rondo in A-minor K.511 ....8.550052

78. Liszt, Dream of Love 8.550052

79. Offenbach, Barcarolle 8.550053

80. Chopin, Prelude No.15 in D flat-major, Op.28, No.15 ....8.550053

TRACK LISTING FOR COMPANION CD

PRELUDE/INTERLUDE/POSTLUDE/INCIDENTAL-CONT'D...

81. Chopin, Etude in E-major, Op.10, No.3 ....8.550218

82. Chopin, Variations on Non piu Mesta 8.550107

83. Beethoven, Andante in F-major 8.550107

84. Beethoven, Menuet in G 8.550216

85. Brahms, Waltz in A-flat 8.550107

86. Saint-Saëns, The Swan 8.550107

87. Mendelssohn, Song Without Words 8.550217

88. Rachmaninov, Vocalise 8.550141

89. Rachmaninov, Rhapsody on a Theme of Paganini 8.550219

90. Debussy, Clair de Lune 8.550141

91. Debussy, Arabesque No. 2 ....8.550218

92. Debussy, Petite Suite (excerpt) for Flute and Harp 8.550741

93. Faure, Berceuse Op.16 ....8.550216

94. Schubert, Impromptu in G flat-major, Op.90, No.3 ....8.550647

95. Grieg, Wedding Day at Troldhaugen, Op.65, No.6 ....8.553252

96. Albeniz, Tango in D-major 8.553252

97. Schumann, Romance Op.94 for Violin and Piano 8.550125

98. Bizet, Adagietto for Violin & Piano (from L'Arlesienne) 8.550125

99. Ravel, Vocalise en forme de habanera 8.550741

CEREMONY MUSIC

MUSIC IS AN IMPORTANT PART OF YOUR CEREMONY, from your first step down the aisle to the moment you are pronounced man and wife! In this chapter you will find explanations of the times when music is used during the ceremony, as well the styles typically used for each one.

PARTS OF THE CEREMONY

- Prelude
- Pre-Processional
- Processional
- Bride's Entrance
- Ceremony
- Unity Candle
- Recessional
- Interlude/Postlude

The tables following each section provide song suggestions; including song name, album name, artist and genre.

PRELUDE

The prelude is the period of time before the ceremony begins. During the prelude your guests will be arriving and taking their seats. You want to make sure that there is music playing as soon as your first guests arrive so you should begin playing your prelude music as early as possible.

Deciding when to start playing the music for your prelude will depend on such things as how long you are allowed to use your ceremony site (one or two hours before the ceremony) and how the prelude music will be provided.

If you have hired musicians that get paid by the hour, you may want your prelude to start later than if you are playing a CD.

Prelude music sets the tone for your wedding and gives your guests their first impression of what type of ceremony to expect. You may choose chamber music pieces for a formal ceremony, or smooth jazz for a less formal ceremony. In general, the music should be non-intrusive.

PRELUDE

MUSIC FOR THE PRELUDE

TITLE COMPOSER/ARTIST	GENRE/STYLE ALBUM
ADAGIO FOR STRINGS, OP.11 Barber	Classical Various
AIR ON A G STRING Bach	Classical 7173
ALL I ASK OF YOU Andrew Lloyd Webber	Musical Phantom of the Opera
AVE VERUM CORPUS Mozart	Choral Various
CAVARELLI RUSTICANA- INTERMEZZO Mascagni	Classical Various
CLAIR DE LUNE Debussy	Classical 8.550141
FOUR SEASONS: WINTER, LARGO Vivaldi	Classical 8.550056
FUR ELISE Beethoven	Classical Various
THE GIFT Jim Brickman	Pop/Piano The Gift
LARGHETTO FROM XERXES Handel	Classical 8.550521

TITLE COMPOSER/ARTIST	GENRE/STYLE ALBUM
PASTORAL SYM: SCENE BY THE BROOK Beethoven	Classical Various
ROMANCE NO. 2 Beethoven	Classical Various
SYM NO 28 ANDANTE Mozart	Classical Various

NOTES:

_____
_____
_____
_____
_____
_____
_____
_____
_____
_____
_____
_____
_____
_____
_____

♫ *Lyrics Provided*

PRE-PROCESSIONAL

SELECTING YOUR PRE-PROCESSIONAL MUSIC

The pre-processional is the time just before the procession of the wedding party begins. This is the time when important family members, such as the mother-of-the-bride, are ushered to their seats. Changing the music from prelude to pre-processional lets your guests know that the ceremony is about to begin and is a way to honor family members who are especially important to you.

The choices for pre-processional music are endless. You may choose a piece of chamber music, an instrumental version of a contemporary ballad, or something that has special meaning to you and your family, such as a version of a lullaby your mother used to sing, or a favorite hymn of your grandmother's. While the choice is yours, keep in mind the tempo of the piece and how it will fit in with your other ceremony musical choices. A song that is vastly different in style from your prelude and processional may make your ceremony music seem disconnected.

MUSIC FOR THE PRE-PROCESSIONAL

TITLE COMPOSER/ARTIST	GENRE/STYLE ALBUM
AIR - WATER MUSIC SUITE Handel	Classical 8.55019
CANZON V Giovanni Gabrieli	Classical 8.553873
EMPEROR'S HYMN Haydn	Classical Various
SON. NO 3 DETTA DEL NICCOLINI Girolamo Fantini	Classical 8.553593
♫ SUNRISE, SUNSET Sheldon Harnick & Jerry Bock	Musical Fiddler on the Roof
TRUMPET VOLUNTARY Jeremiah Clarke	Classical 8.550790

TITLE COMPOSER/ARTIST	GENRE/STYLE ALBUM
"WINTER" LARGO, FOUR SEASONS Vivaldi	Classical 8.55319-20

NOTES:

_____

_____

_____

_____

_____

_____

_____

_____

_____

♫ *Lyrics Provided*

PROCESSIONAL AND BRIDE'S ENTRANCE

SELECTING YOUR PROCESSIONAL AND BRIDE'S ENTRANCE MUSIC

Processional music is played as the bridal party walks down the aisle. When the wedding party appears at the top of the aisle, the music should switch from pre-processional to processional. The processional piece should have a tempo that allows the bridesmaids and groomsmen to walk down the aisle at a measured pace and heightens the suspense for the wedding guests as they wait to see the bride. Many people use classical pieces for this part of the ceremony. When choosing a piece, keep in mind how the music will be played. A piece that is perfect in full orchestral form may not have the same presence if performed by a string quartet.

As soon as the bride appears at the top of the aisle, the music should switch to the piece you have chosen for the bride's entrance. This is the moment that you, and all of your guests, have been waiting for. Your music should be dramatic and sweeping. Feel free to consider music besides the traditional wedding march, such as instrumental versions of favorite ballads and contemporary love songs. Keep in mind the tempo and how the piece will be performed.

MUSIC FOR THE PROCESSIONAL AND BRIDE'S ENTRANCE

TITLE COMPOSER/ARTIST	GENRE/STYLE ALBUM	TITLE COMPOSER/ARTIST	GENRE/STYLE ALBUM
AIR *(From Water Music)* Handel	Classical 8.550109	LARGHETTO *(From Xerxes)* Handel	Classical 8.550521
BRIDAL CHORUS Wagner	Classical 8.550790	OBOE CONCERTO *(Slow Movement)* Handel	Classical 8.550102
CANON IN D Pachelbel	Classical 8.550790	OVERTURE *(From Royal Fireworks Music)* Handel	Classical 8.550109
CANZON V Giovanni Gabrieli	Classical 8.553873	PATHETIQUE SONATA Beethoven	Classical 8.550045
GUITAR CONCERTO IN D MAJOR Vivaldi	Classical 8.550274	PROMENADE *(From Pictures at an Exhibition)* Mussorgsky	Classical 8.553249
GYMNOPEDIE NO.1 Satie	Classical 8.554166	SEE THE CONQU'ING HERO Handel	Classical 8.556665

♪ *Lyrics Provided*

PROCESSIONAL AND BRIDE'S ENTRANCE

MUSIC FOR THE PROCESSIONAL AND BRIDE'S ENTRANCE

TITLE COMPOSER/ARTIST	GENRE/STYLE ALBUM
SONATAS FOR ORGAN, OP. 65, NO. 3	Classical
Mendelssohn	8.553583
TE DEUM	Classical
Charpentier	8.550581
TO A WILD ROSE	Classical
MacDowell	8.559010
TOCCATA (From L'Orfeo)	Classical
Monteverdi	8.554094-95
TRUMPET CONCERTO IN D (IV-Allegro)	Classical
Telemann	8.553531
TRUMPET TUNE	Classical
Purcell	8.550790
TRUMPET VOLUNTARY	Classical
Clarke	8.550790
WINTER, LARGO	Classical
Vivaldi	8.550056

NOTES:

♫ *Lyrics Provided*

CEREMONY AND UNITY CANDLE

SELECTING YOUR CEREMONY AND UNITY CANDLE MUSIC

Using music during your ceremony is a personal choice. Some couples may have favorite songs playing softly as background music throughout the ceremony, while others may take a break in the ceremony to have a favorite hymn sung in place of a reading. Others opt to have no music at all. Whether or not you have music during the ceremony may depend on where your wedding is taking place. Some churches and other religious establishments may have restrictions on what music can be played during a religious service. Make sure to inquire about this.

A special part of many ceremonies is the lighting of the unity candle. The bride and the groom each use a lit candle to light the unity candle which symbolizes two becoming one. The candle has no religious significance so can be used in ceremonies of every denomination. Many couples chose to set the lighting of their unity candle to music. You may want to consider having a favorite song or a special hymn to play as background music, or having a vocalist perform a song that has significance to you as a couple. Again, be sure to check with the wedding coordinator at your ceremony site to determine if there are any restrictions on what music is allowed.

MUSIC FOR THE CEREMONY AND LIGHTING OF THE UNITY CANDLE

TITLE	GENRE/STYLE	TITLE	GENRE/STYLE
COMPOSER/ARTIST	ALBUM	COMPOSER/ARTIST	ALBUM
ALL PEOPLE ON EARTH DO DWELL	Hymn	THE WEDDING SONG (*There Is Love*)	Pop Vocal
Various	Various	Petula Clark	These Are My Songs
AMAZING GRACE	Gospel	THE WEDDING SONG	Hymn
Mahalia Jackson	For Collectors Only	The Lennon Sisters	22 Songs of Faith...
AVE MARIA	Classical	YOU ARE THE ONE	Classic Pop Vocals
Shubert	8.553751	Debbie Friedman	It's You
BEAUTIFUL IN MY EYES	Pop Vocal	NOTES:	
Joshua Kadison	Painted Desert Serenade		
BECAUSE WE ARE IN LOVE	Pop Vocal		
The Carpenters	Made In America		
MORNING HAS BROKEN	Hymn		
Eleanor Farjeon	Various		

♫ *Lyrics Provided*

RECESSIONAL

SELECTING YOUR RECESSIONAL MUSIC

As soon as you are pronounced husband and wife your recessional music will begin. This is the moment you and your new spouse will walk back up the aisle. You should choose music that is joyous and conveys your feelings of excitement and happiness.

There is an unlimited variety of classical and contemporary music to choose from - everything from a traditional wedding march to a contemporary pop song. Use this time to create a feeling of celebration, but consider how your musical choice will be performed, what is appropriate for your ceremony site and how formal your wedding is.

MUSIC FOR THE RECESSIONAL

TITLE COMPOSER/ARTIST	GENRE/STYLE ALBUM
ARRIVAL OF THE QUEEN OF SHEBA	Classical
Handel	8.556665
BRANDENBURG CONCERTO NO.4, ALLEGRO	Classical
Bach	8.554608
CONCERTO FOR TWO TRUMPETS IN B- ALLEGRO	Classical
Vivaldi	8.550014
CROWN IMPERIAL	Classical
Walton	8.553981
FUGUE IN E-FLAT MAJOR	Classical
Mendelssohn	8.550184
HALLELUJAH CHORUS *(From the Messiah)*	Classical
Handel	8.550779
HORNPIPE *(From Water Music)*	Classical
Handel	8.550109

TITLE COMPOSER/ARTIST	GENRE/STYLE ALBUM
HORNPIPE *(From Concerto Grosso OP. 6, No. 7)*	Classical
Handel	8.550102
ODE TO JOY	Classical
Beethoven	8.556623
SPRING, ALLEGRO *(The Four Seasons)*	Classical
Vivaldi	8.555319-20
TOCCATA	Classical
Widor	8.550790
TRUMPET CONCERTO IN B, ALLEGRO	Classical
Telemann	8.550104
TRUMPET CONCERTO IN D, II ALLEGRO	Classical
Telemann	8.553531
WEDDING MARCH	Classical
Mendelssohn	8.550790

♫ *Lyrics Provided*

INTERLUDE/POSTLUDE

SELECTING YOUR INTERLUDE/POSTLUDE MUSIC

The interlude or postlude, is the time between the end of the ceremony and the beginning of the reception. Many couples use this time to take wedding party pictures or to greet their guests in a receiving line. The music you choose for the interlude should be non-intrusive to allow for conversation while your guests mingle and enjoy refreshments and hors d'oeuvres. You may choose to have smooth jazz, a string quartet, or a CD of instrumental or New Age music playing.

If you have hired a band, be sure that they perform at an appropriate volume for the interlude and avoid songs with vocals unless they are performing far from the receiving line. The interlude may be a good time to showcase you and your fiance's musical tastes.

MUSIC FOR THE INTERLUDE/POSTLUDE

TITLE COMPOSER/ARTIST	GENRE/STYLE ALBUM	TITLE COMPOSER/ARTIST	GENRE/STYLE ALBUM
"ALLELUIA" *(From Exsultate Jubilate)* Mozart	Classical 8.550495	MINUET IN G Beethoven	Classical 8.550216
ARABESQUE Debussy	Classical 8.554166	MUSETTA'S WALTZ, LA BOHEME Puccini	Classical 8.553751
AVE MARIA Schubert	Classical 8.553151	PASTORAL SYMPHONY Handel	Classical 8.556665
CARILLON DE WESTMINSTER Vierne	Classical 8.550955	WALTZ IN A FLAT Brahms	Classical 8.550107
CLAIRE DE LUNE Debussy	Classical 8.550141	NOTES:	
GREENSLEEVES Traditional	Classical 8.550141		
JESU, JOY OF MAN'S DESIRING Bach	Classical 8.556656		

♪ *Lyrics Provided*

RECEPTION MUSIC

MUSIC FOR YOUR RECEPTION GOES BEYOND just choosing something with a nice beat you can dance to. Throughout the reception there will be times when you want to hear a specific song. Select music that will be appropriate for the formality of your reception and related to the mood and ambience you wish to create.

PARTS OF THE RECEPTION:

- Cocktail Hour
- Newlyweds' Entrance
- During Dinner
- First Dance
- Family Dances
- Toasts
- Bouquet Toss
- Garter Removal and Toss
- Cake Cutting
- Money Dance
- Ethnic Dances
- Last Dance

Some of the following sections contain tables providing song suggestions for popular music used during the different phases of the wedding reception. The tables provide the song name, album name, artist and genre.

In the back of the book, you will find the lyrics to 100 of the most popular wedding songs today. Songs with lyrics provided are noted on the tables by the symbol "♫"

COCKTAIL HOUR

The cocktail hour may or may not be an extension of your postlude, depending on how and where you have your reception. If your guests have traveled to a new location, you may want to change the style of your music to reflect a more party-like atmosphere. You may want to choose background music that can be played as your guests mingle around the bar and cocktail area. Smooth jazz, instrumental versions of pop songs, string quartets playing classical pieces, or a band playing low-key jazz standards are all good choices for the cocktail hour.

NEWLYWEDS' ENTRANCE

The entrance of the bride and groom to the reception is the first time that you will be introduced to your family and friends as husband and wife. This is a grand entrance, so choose music that fits the moment. There are numerous choices for for classical music that will create a feeling of celebration. For less formal receptions, you may want to choose popular rock or R&B songs. Because the song will most likely not play long (you will soon change to the music for your first dance) you have the freedom to choose a song that has a great chorus, even if you do not want the rest of the song played.

DURING DINNER

If you are serving a meal during the reception, you should decide what type of music to play while your guests dine. Follow the same rule of thumb that you would for the cocktail hour; in other words, background music that sets the mood for your reception. If you have hired a harpist or string quartet for your ceremony, consider having them perform throughout the dinner hour as well. Smooth Jazz, New Age and Easy Listening are all good choices. If a DJ is providing your music, be sure they keep music at an appropriate volume.

THE FIRST DANCE

The First Dance is probably the most romantic moment of your reception and choosing the right song can be the easiest or most difficult musical choice you will have to make. If you and your spouse have a song that has special meaning for you, this is the perfect time to play it. If you do not have something already picked out, you will want to choose a song that conveys the feelings and thoughts you have about each other and your marriage. Start by using the list of first dance songs found in this section.

These are some of the most requested first dance songs across the country. You may also want to listen to a radio station that specializes in love songs or ballads, or ask your wedding consultant, DJ or bandleader for more suggestions.

The key to picking the perfect first dance song is to listen to as many different songs as possible and work with your fiancé to narrow down the list to a few favorites. If you and your fiancé have specific musical tastes, or favorite genres, that may be a great way to start the selection process. The most important thing to keep in mind is this: your First Dance is a special dance that celebrates your marriage, so choose music that you both love!

SONGS FOR THE FIRST DANCE

TITLE	GENRE/STYLE
COMPOSER/ARTIST	ALBUM
A WHOLE NEW WORLD	R&B
Peabo Bryson & Regina Belle	Disney's Aladdin
♫ AFTER ALL	Pop
Cher	Heart of Stone
ALL MY LIFE	R&B
K-Ci & JoJo	Love Always
♫ ALWAYS	R&B
Atlantic Starr	Ultimate Collection
ALWAYS	Jazz Vocals
Sarah Vaughn & Billy Eckstein	1944-1946
♫ AMAZED	Country
Lonestar	Lonely Grill
ANNIE'S SONG	Folk
John Denver Reflections: Songs of Love and Life	
AS TIME GOES BY	Jazz Vocals
Tony Bennett	Classic Tony Bennett 2
AT LAST	R&B
Etta James	Her Best
BEAUTIFUL	Folk
Gordon Lightfoot	Gord's Gold
♫ BECAUSE YOU LOVED ME	Pop
Celine Dion Up Close & Personal Soundtrack	

TITLE	GENRE/STYLE
COMPOSER/ARTIST	ALBUM
♫ BEST THING THAT EVER	R&B
HAPPENED TO ME	
Gladys Knight & The Pips	Greatest Hits
CAN YOU FEEL THE	Pop
LOVE TONIGHT	
Elton John	Love Songs
CAN'T HELP FALLING IN LOVE	Classic Pop
Elvis Presley	Heart & Soul
CHANCES ARE	Easy Listening
Johnny Mathis	Johnny's Greatest Hits
CLOSE TO YOU	Pop
Carpenters	Close to You
CRAZY	Country
Patsy Cline	Heartaches
CRAZY FOR YOU	Pop
Madonna	Something to Remember
DON'T KNOW MUCH	Pop
Linda Ronstadt,	
Aaron Neville	Cry Like A Rainstorm
DREAMING OF YOU	Tejano
Selena	Dreaming of You
♫ ENDLESS LOVE	R&B
Lionel Richie (with Diana Ross)	Back to Front

♫ *Lyrics Provided*

FIRST DANCE

SONGS FOR THE FIRST DANCE

TITLE COMPOSER/ARTIST	GENRE/STYLE ALBUM
ETERNAL FLAME Bangles	Pop Greatest Hits
EVERY BREATH YOU TAKE Police	Pop Every Breath You Take: The Classics
(*Everything I Do*) I DO IT FOR YOU Bryan Adams	Pop So Far, So Good
♫ FOR YOU I WILL Monica	R&B The Boy Is Mine
FOREVER AND EVER, AMEN Randy Travis	Country Greatest #1 Hits
♫ FROM THIS MOMENT ON Shania Twain & Brian White	Country/Pop Come On Over
GROW OLD WITH ME Mary Chapin Carpenter	Country Party Doll & Other Favorites
HAVE I TOLD YOU LATELY Rod Stewart	Pop Unplugged
♫ HAVE YOU EVER REALLY LOVED A WOMAN Bryan Adams	Pop Don Juan DeMarco
♫ HOLD ME Teddy Pendergrass	R & B Love Language

TITLE COMPOSER/ARTIST	GENRE/STYLE ALBUM
I DO, CHERISH YOU Mark Wills	Country Wish You Were Here
I DON'T WANT TO MISS A THING Aerosmith	Pop Armageddon the Soundtrack
♫ I FINALLY FOUND Barbra Streisand & Bryan Adams	Pop All Time Greatest Movie Songs
I GET A KICK OUT OF YOU Frank Sinatra	Classic Pop Vocals Gold
I GIVE MY HEART John Berry	Country Faces
♫ I HONESTLY LOVE YOU Olivia Newton-John	Pop Back to Basics
♫ I ONLY HAVE EYES FOR YOU The Flamingos	Oldies Best of the Flamingos
♫ I SWEAR All-4-One	Pop All-4-One
IF Bread	Classic Soft Rock Retrospective
I'LL STAND BY YOU The Pretenders	Pop Last of the Independents

♫ *Lyrics Provided*

FIRST DANCE

SONGS FOR THE FIRST DANCE

TITLE COMPOSER/ARTIST	GENRE/STYLE ALBUM
IN MY LIFE Beatles	Pop Rubber Soul
IN YOUR EYES Peter Gabriel	Pop So
IT HAD TO BE YOU Harry Connick Jr.	Jazz Vocals When Harry Met Sally Soundtrack
IT'S YOUR LOVE Faith Hill & Tim McGraw	Country Tim McGraw Greatest Hits
JUST THE WAY YOU ARE Billy Joel	Pop The Stranger
♫ LADY Kenny Rogers	Country Greatest Country Hits
LET'S STAY TOGETHER Al Green	R&B Greatest Hits
♫ LOVE, ME Collin Raye	Country Love Songs
ME AND YOU Kenny Chesney	Country Me and You
NOBODY LOVES ME LIKE YOU DO Anne Murray	Pop The Best (So Far)

TITLE COMPOSER/ARTIST	GENRE/STYLE ALBUM
THE ONE Elton John	Pop Love Songs
OUR LOVE IS HERE TO STAY Billie Holiday	Jazz Vocals The Silver Collection
PERHAPS LOVE Placido Domingo & John Denver	Pop Vocals The Domingo Songbook
SAY YOU SAY ME Lionel Richie	R&B Back to Front
SENTIMENTAL JOURNEY Doris Day	Classic Pop Vocals Sentimental Journey
SHE'S GOT A WAY Billy Joel	Pop Songs in the Attic
SOME ENCHANTED EVENING Original Cast	Musical South Pacific Soundtrack
SPEND MY LIFE WITH YOU Eric Benet (with Tamia)	R&B A Day in the Life
TAKE MY BREATH AWAY Berlin	Pop Best of Berlin 1979-1988
TO LOVE SOMEBODY Michael Bolton	Pop Vocals Timeless: The Classics

♫ *Lyrics Provided*

FIRST DANCE

SONGS FOR THE FIRST DANCE

TITLE COMPOSER/ARTIST	GENRE/STYLE ALBUM
TO MAKE YOU FEEL MY LOVE Garth Brooks	Country Fresh Horses
TONIGHT AND FOREVER Carly Simon	Pop Vocals Spoiled Girl
TRUE COMPANION Marc Cohn	Pop Marc Cohn
TRULY MADLY DEEPLY Savage Garden	Pop Savage Garden
UNCHAINED MELODY Righteous Brothers	Oldies The Very Best of the Righteous Brothers
UNEXPECTED SONG Bernadette Peters	Vocal Mr. Producer
VALENTINE Martina McBride & Jim Brickman	New Age Picture This
♫ THE WAY YOU LOOK TONIGHT Tony Bennett	Jazz Vocals My Best Friend's Wedding
THE WEDDING SONG *(There is Love)* Petula Clark	Pop Just Petula
♫ WE'VE ONLY JUST BEGUN Carpenters	Pop Close to You

TITLE COMPOSER/ARTIST	GENRE/STYLE ALBUM
♫ WHEN A MAN LOVES A WOMAN Michael Bolton	Pop Time, Love and Tenderness
♫ WHEN I FALL IN LOVE Nat King Cole	Classic Pop Vocals More Sleepless Nights
♫ WHEN I SAID I DO Clint Black	Country D'lectrified
WONDERFUL TONIGHT Eric Clapton	Pop Cream of Clapton
YOU AND I Crystal Gayle and Eddie Rabbit	Country Greatest Hits
♫ YOU ARE SO BEAUTIFUL Joe Cocker	Pop Greatest Hits
YOU DECORATED MY LIFE Kenny Rogers	Country Always In Love
♫ YOU'RE STILL THE ONE Shania Twain	Country Come on Over
♫ YOU'RE THE INSPIRATION Chicago	Pop Chicago 17

NOTES:

_____

_____

_____

♫ *Lyrics Provided*

SELECTING SONGS FOR YOUR FAMILY DANCES

After you and your new spouse have had your First Dance, it is customary to invite other family members to share a dance with the bride and the groom. Traditionally there is a bride and father-of-the-bride dance, and a groom and mother-of-the-groom dance. You can have these dances simultaneously or separately, depending on your preference and the formality of your reception.

The music for these dances can be a favorite song of one of the parents, a meaningful popular song, or the instrumental version of a song that has special meaning about one of the parents, such as a lullaby your father or mother used to use to sing. This dance is an opportunity to give your parents special recognition and to thank them for their love and support through the years, so choose something they will like and appreciate.

You may also want to consider having more family dances to include step-parents, grandparents and even mentors that are special to you and your fiancé. You do not have to dance with the same family member through the whole song. If there are others you wish to recognize with a special dance, change partners midway through the music.

SONGS FOR THE FATHER-DAUGHTER DANCE

TITLE	GENRE/STYLE		TITLE	GENRE/STYLE
COMPOSER/ARTIST	ALBUM		COMPOSER/ARTIST	ALBUM
A SMILE LIKE YOURS	R&B		DADDY'S HANDS	Country
Natalie Cole	A Smile Like Yours (soundtrack)			Milestones:
			Holly Dunn	Greatest Hits
♫ ALL I HAVE	Country		FATHER-DAUGHTER	Contemp. Christian
Beth Neilsen Chapman	Greatest Hits		HARMONY	
			Phil Keaggy	Way Back Home
BUTTERFLY KISSES	Pop			
Bob Carlisle	Butterfly Kisses		FATHER'S EYES	Contemp. Christian
			Amy Grant	My Father's Eyes
CAN YOU FEEL THE LOVE TONIGHT	Pop			
Elton John	Love Songs		HERO	R&B
			Mariah Carey	#1s
CHILD OF MINE	Pop Vocal			
Carole King	Writer: Carole King		IN MY LIFE	Pop
				Imagine
DADDY'S GIRL	Pop			(Soundtrack)
Peter Cetera	Solitude/Solitaire		John Lennon	

♫ *Lyrics Provided*

FAMILY DANCES

SONGS FOR THE FATHER-DAUGHTER DANCE

TITLE COMPOSER/ARTIST	GENRE/STYLE ALBUM
ISN'T SHE LOVELY Stevie Wonder	R&B A Smile Like Yours (Soundtrack)
LULLABY Billy Joel	Pop Greatest Hits, Vol. 3
ME AND MY FATHER Cosy Sheridan	Pop Saturn Return
MY FATHER Nina Simone	Jazz Vocals Baltimore
MY FUNNY VALENTINE Chet Baker	Jazz Vocals My Funny Valentine
MY GIRL The Temptations	R&B Oldies My Girl
THANK HEAVEN FOR LITTLE GIRLS Maurice Chevalier	Musical Gigi (Soundtrack)
THROUGH THE YEARS Kenny Rogers	Country 20 Greatest Hits
UNFORGETTABLE Natalie Cole & Nat King Cole	Classic Pop Vocals Unforgettable
♫ THE WAY YOU LOOK TONIGHT Frank Sinatra	Classic Pop Vocal Sings Days of Wine and Roses

TITLE COMPOSER/ARTIST	GENRE/STYLE ALBUM
WHAT A WONDERFUL WORLD Louis Armstrong	Jazz All Time Greatest Hits
YOUR SMILING FACE James Taylor	Pop Greatest Hits, Vol. 2

NOTES:

_____
_____
_____
_____
_____
_____
_____
_____
_____
_____
_____
_____
_____
_____
_____
_____
_____

♫ *Lyrics Provided*

FAMILY DANCES

SONGS FOR THE MOTHER-SON DANCE

TITLE COMPOSER/ARTIST	GENRE/STYLE ALBUM
♫ ALL THE THINGS YOU ARE Tony Bennett	Jazz At Carnegie Hall
BECAUSE YOU LOVED ME Celine Dion	Pop Up Close and Personal (Soundtrack)
BLESSED Elton John	Pop Love Songs
♫ DEARLY BELOVED Dinah Shore	Classic Pop Vocals Buttons and Bows
♫ FOR ALL WE KNOW Carpenters	Vocal Carpenters
HAVE I TOLD YOU LATELY THAT I LOVE YOU Bing Crosby & Andrews Sisters	Classic Pop Their Complete Recordings
I AM YOUR CHILD Barry Manilow	Pop Vocals Barry Manilow I
I HAD A GOOD MOTHER AND FATHER Kate Wolf	Folk Looking Back At You
♫ I WISH YOU LOVE Natalie Cole	R&B Take A Look
IN THIS LIFE Bette Midler	Pop Vocal Bette of Roses

TITLE COMPOSER/ARTIST	GENRE/STYLE ALBUM
♫ LONG AGO (And Far Away) Gail Marten	Jazz Beyond the Rainbow
MAKE SOMEONE HAPPY Jimmy Durante	Classic Pop Vocals As Time Goes By: The Best of Jimmy Durante
MOON RIVER Andy Williams	Classic Pop Vocals Music of Henry Mancini
STAND BY ME Ben E King	R&B Oldies Stand By Me & Other Hits
♫ SUNRISE, SUNSET Original Cast	Musical Fiddler on the Roof (Soundtrack)
'TIL THE END OF TIME Perry Como	Classic Pop Vocals TV Favorites
♫ WIND BENEATH MY WINGS Bette Midler	Pop Experience the Divine
YOU ARE THE SUNSHINE OF MY LIFE Stevie Wonder	R&B Motown Year by Year: 1973
♫ YOU LIGHT UP MY LIFE Debby Boone	Gospel Best Of
YOU'VE GOT A FRIEND James Taylor	Pop Greatest Hits vol.1

♫ *Lyrics Provided*

TOASTS

SELECTING SONGS FOR YOUR TOASTS

Another highlight of your reception will be the toasts. Traditionally the best man and the maid of honor will toast the bride and groom at the beginning of the reception. They may toast shortly after the first dance, just before the meal is served or during the actual meal.

You can choose to have music playing softly in the background for your toasts, acting as a soundtrack to the speeches. You might want to have instrumental versions of songs that celebrate friendship, such as "That's What Friends Are For" or "Stand By Me." Or you may choose to have a favorite piece of classical music performed.

If you went to school with the maid of honor or best man, consider having your school song playing, or your sorority or fraternity's song. Whatever music you choose, be sure it is played at a low enough volume so your guests can easily hear the toasts.

SONGS FOR TOASTS

TITLE COMPOSER/ARTIST	GENRE/STYLE ALBUM	TITLE COMPOSER/ARTIST	GENRE/STYLE ALBUM
♫ ALL THE MAN THAT I NEED Whitney Houston	Pop Greatest Hits	♫ I PLEDGE MY LOVE Peaches & Herb	Pop Wedding Songs
♫ DOIN' IT ALL FOR MY BABY Huey Lewis & The News	Rock Best Of	SHOWER THE PEOPLE James Taylor	Pop Greatest Hits vol. 1
ENJOY IT! Maurice Chevalier	Musical Classic Disney Collection	THAT'S WHAT FRIENDS ARE FOR Dionne Warwick	R&B Greatest Hits (1979-1990)
EVERYTHING IS BEAUTIFUL Foster & Allen	Easy Listening By Request	THESE ARE THE DAYS 10,000 Maniacs	Pop MTV Unplugged
FRIENDS Elton John	Pop Rare Masters	♫ SACRED EMOTION Donny Osmond	Pop Greatest Hits
♫ THE GREATEST LOVE OF ALL Whitney Houston	R&B Whitney Houston	♫ YOUR SONG Elton John	Pop Elton John

♫ *Lyrics Provided*

SELECTING SONGS FOR YOUR BOUQUET TOSS

A popular tradition at many receptions is the bouquet toss. This is when the single women at the wedding get together and the bride tosses her bouquet over her shoulder toward the group. The woman who catches the bouquet is said to be the next to marry.

This tradition is meant to be fun, so choose music that keeps with the theme. Upbeat tempos and lively songs are the perfect choice for the bouquet toss.

SONGS FOR THE BOUQUET TOSS

TITLE / COMPOSER/ARTIST	GENRE/STYLE / ALBUM
AMERICAN WOMAN / Lenny Kravitz	Rock / Austin Powers, Soundtrack
♫ AND I LOVE YOU SO / Don McLean	Rock / Best Of
BEAUTIFUL BOUQUET / The Cox Family	Bluegrass / Beyond the City
BOLD SOUL SISTER / Ike & Tina Turner	Classic R&B / ABC's of Soul vol.2
CELEBRATION / Kool & the Gang	R&B / Celebrate
GIRLS JUST WANT TO HAVE FUN / Cyndi Lauper	Pop / She's So Unusual
I AM WOMAN / Helen Reddy	Pop Vocals / The Essential Helen Reddy Collection
JUMP (For My Love) / Pointer Sisters	R&B / Billboard's Top Hits 1984

TITLE / COMPOSER/ARTIST	GENRE/STYLE / ALBUM
♫ L-O-V-E / Al Green	R&B / Deep Shade of Green
MAN, I FEEL LIKE A WOMAN / Shania Twain	Country / Come On Over
SISTERS ARE DOIN' IT FOR THEMSELVES / The Eurythmics	Pop / Greatest Hits
♫ THE WAY HE MAKES ME FEEL / Barbra Streisand	Vocal / Yentl Soundtrack

NOTES:

_____
_____
_____

_____
_____
_____
_____

_____
_____

♫ *Lyrics Provided*

THE GARTER REMOVAL AND TOSS

SELECTING SONGS FOR THE GARTER REMOVAL AND TOSS

The tradition of the garter toss started as a way to prove that a couple had consummated their marriage. The couple's consummation would be witnessed and as proof, the garter would be brought out of the wedding chamber and shown to the guests.

Today the groom removes the garter and tosses it over his shoulder to a group of single men. The garter toss is also a fun tradition that deserves a great song. Your choices range from the instrumental "The Stripper" to ZZ Top's "Legs." Keep in mind how formal your reception is, but feel free to be as campy as you think is appropriate.

SONGS FOR THE GARTER REMOVAL AND TOSS

TITLE COMPOSER/ARTIST	GENRE/STYLE ALBUM
ANOTHER ONE BITES THE DUST Queen	Rock Greatest Hits (Hollywood)
♫ BABY, I LOVE YOUR WAY Big Mountain	Reggae Unity
♫ CAN I STEAL A LITTLE LOVE Frank Sinatra	Jazz Capitol Collector's Series
♫ HEAVEN Bryan Adams	Pop Reckless
♫ HEAVEN MUST BE MISSING AN ANGEL Tavares	Disco Charlie's Angels Soundtrack
♫ EBB TIDE Tom Jones	Vocal Collector's Edition
FEVER Peggy Lee	Classic Pop Vocals All Time Greatest Hits, Vol. 1

TITLE COMPOSER/ARTIST	GENRE/STYLE ALBUM
♫ IF I EVER FALL IN LOVE Shai	R&B If I Ever Fall in Love
KISS Prince	R&B The Hits 2
LET'S GET IT ON Marvin Gaye	R&B I Heard It Through the Grapevine
♫ LOVE IS ALIVE Gary Wright	Pop Dream Weaver
♫ MAKIN' WHOOPEE Dr. John	Jazz Sleepless in Seattle
OH, PRETTY WOMAN Roy Orbison	Rock Superhits
OH YEAH Yello	Synth Pop Essential

♫ *Lyrics Provided*

THE GARTER REMOVAL AND TOSS

SONGS FOR THE GARTER REMOVAL AND TOSS

TITLE	GENRE/STYLE
COMPOSER/ARTIST	ALBUM
SHAMELESS	Country
Garth Brooks	Ropin' the Wind
♫ STAND BY YOUR MAN	Country
Tammy Wynette	Greatest Hits
THE STRIPPER	Lounge
David Rose	Bachelor Pad
& His Orchestra	Pleasures
♫ SWEET NOTHIN'S	Country
Brenda Lee	Anthology
THEME FROM	TV theme
MISSION IMPOSSIBLE	
Larry Mullen/Adam Clayton	Mission Impossible
WILD THING	Rap
Tone-Loc	Hard Rock Café: Party Classics
YOU SEXY THING	R&B
Hot Chocolate	14 Greatest Hits
♫ (You've Got) PERSONALITY	Rock
Mitch Ryder	All Hits

NOTES:

♫ *Lyrics Provided*

THE CAKE CUTTING

SELECTING SONGS FOR THE CAKE CUTTING

The wedding cake goes back as far as the ancient Romans who used a cake made of wheat flour, water and salt during marriage ceremonies. The wedding cake has come a long way since then and now the cake cutting is a traditional part of most receptions.

The first cut is made by both the bride and the groom. Together, they hold the cake-cutting knife and cut the first slice. This act is meant to symbolize the bride and groom's shared future. The cake cutting is often set to music, and in fact your DJ or Emcee will signal to your guests that the cake cutting is going to take place by changing music.

Once again, keep in mind how formal your reception is when picking the music for this tradition. As with the other parts of your wedding, this is a celebratory moment so have fun with the music!

SONGS FOR THE CAKE CUTTING

TITLE COMPOSER/ARTIST	GENRE/STYLE ALBUM
♫ ALL I DO IS DREAM OF YOU	Vocal
Dean Martin	The Capitol Years
APPETITE FOR LOVE	Blues
Sy Klopps	Berkley Soul
♫ CAN'T SMILE WITHOUT YOU	Vocal
Carpenters	A Kind of Hush
CHAPEL OF LOVE	Pop Vocals
Bette Midler	The Divine Miss M
♫ COMPLETELY	Pop
Michael Bolton	One Thing
FOR YOUR SWEET LOVE	Oldies
Rick Nelson	For Your Sweet Love

TITLE COMPOSER/ARTIST	GENRE/STYLE ALBUM
HE'S SURE THE BOY I LOVE	Motown
Darlene Love	The Best of Darlene Love
HOW SWEET IT IS *(To Be Loved By You)*	Pop
James Taylor	Greatest Hits
I GOT YOU BABE	Pop
Sonny and Cher	Good Times
♫ I LOVE YOU TOO MUCH	Big Band
Andrews Sisters	Rarities
♫ I ONLY HAVE EYES FOR YOU	Vocal
Doris Day	Que Sera Sera
♫ IF YOU SAY MY EYES ARE BEAUTIFUL	R&B
Whitney Houston	Greatest Hits

♫ *Lyrics Provided*

THE CAKE CUTTING

SONGS FOR THE CAKE CUTTING

TITLE COMPOSER/ARTIST	GENRE/STYLE ALBUM
JOY TO THE WORLD Three Dog Night	Rock 20th Century Masters
♫ LOOK HEART, NO HANDS Randy Travis	Country Greatest Hits, Vol. 2
♫ LOVE AND MARRIAGE Frank Sinatra	Classic Pop Vocals The Very Good Years
OH HAPPY DAY Joan Baez	Folk Greatest Hits
RECIPE FOR LOVE Harry Connick Jr.	Jazz Vocals We Are In Love
RECIPE FOR MY LOVE Danny Jennsen	Bubblegum Pop Scooby-Doo's Snack Tracks
SUGAR, SUGAR Archies	Oldies The Very Best of the Archies
♫ SOMEWHERE OUT THERE Linda Ronstadt w/James Ingram	Pop American Tail
♫ THIS GUY'S IN LOVE WITH YOU Herb Albert	Easy Listening Foursider

NOTES:

♫ *Lyrics Provided*

THE MONEY DANCE

SELECTING SONGS FOR THE MONEY DANCE

The Money Dance, or Dollar Dance, is a tradition that is alive and well. Originally a Polish tradition, this dance has made its way into American weddings in various parts of the country. It is a way for the bride and groom to make a little extra money for their honeymoon or for starting their new life together.

The dance is traditionally started with the bride and the best man. While they dance, the best man pins a dollar to the bride's dress, or places it in a small satin purse the bride carries. Guests are then invited to "pay" for dances with the bride by pinning dollars on her or placing them in her purse. While there is no obligation for the guests to take part in this tradition, many guests do find the Money Dance a fun way to help the couple pay their expenses.

The musical choices for a Money Dance are varied. You can choose music that is simply fun to dance to or go with songs that have a money theme.

SONGS FOR THE MONEY DANCE

TITLE COMPOSER/ARTIST	GENRE/STYLE ALBUM	TITLE COMPOSER/ARTIST	GENRE/STYLE ALBUM
10 CENTS A DANCE Nancye Hayes	Pop Vocal At the School of the Arts Café	THE MAGIC PENNY Cathy Fink	Children's When the Rain Comes Down
BETCHA NICKEL Ella Fitzgerald	Jazz Ken Burns Jazz: Ella Fitzgerald	MATERIAL GIRL Madonna	Pop Immaculate Collection
COINS AND PROMISES Margaret Becker	Contemp. Christian Falling Forward	MONEY BLUES Louie Armstrong	Jazz Instrumental His Best Recordings...
FOR LOVE OF MONEY O'Jay	R&B/Funk Old School Funk II	MONEY HONEY Elvis Presley	Pop Elvis '56
GOT A PENNY Nat King Cole	Classic Jazz Vocals 1941-1943	MONEY, MONEY, MONEY Abba	Pop Abba: Gold
I NEED SOME MONEY John Lee Hooker	Blues That's My Story	MONEY (That's What I Want) Beatles	Pop With the Beatles

♬ *Lyrics Provided*

SONGS FOR THE MONEY DANCE

| TITLE | GENRE/STYLE |
COMPOSER/ARTIST	ALBUM
MONEY *(Tired of Working)*	Pop
Steve Bassett	Standing on the Verge
PENNIES FROM HEAVEN	Jazz vocals
Billie Holiday	Ladies of Jazz Disc 1
PENNY FOR YOUR THOUGHTS	R&B
Tavares	Check It Out
PRIVATE DANCER	R&B
Tina Turner	Simply the Best
SHE WORKS HARD FOR HER MONEY	R&B
Donna Summer	Greatest Hits
THREE COINS	Classic Pop Vocals
IN A FOUNTAIN	The Four Aces
Four Aces	Greatest Hits

NOTES:

♫ *Lyrics Provided*

ETHNIC DANCES

SELECTING SONGS FOR ETHNIC DANCES

Your wedding is the perfect time to celebrate your culture and heritage. Whether you and your fiancé share the same heritage, or your marriage is a melding of different ethnicities, you can highlight and honor your cultures through music.

Even if you are hosting a traditional American wedding, there is room for ethnic dancing at your reception. Some cultures have traditional songs and dances that are played at all weddings, for others, simply playing ethnic music is enough to pay homage to your heritage.

Jewish, Irish and Polish weddings have traditional songs and dances. For other cultures that do not have a specific wedding song or dance, have your band or DJ play some traditional music. Be prepared to provide a CD or sheet music, because many musicians will not have a variety of ethnic music to choose from.

SONGS FOR ETHNIC DANCES

TITLE COMPOSER/ARTIST	GENRE/STYLE ALBUM	TITLE COMPOSER/ARTIST	GENRE/STYLE ALBUM
4 WEDDING POLKAS Trebunia Family Band	Polish … Tatra Mountains	GRANADA Jose Carreras	Latin Essential
BASHANA Shlomit	Jewish Songs In Hebrew	HAVA NAGILA Danny Albert	Jewish Music for a Jewish Wedding
HASTE TO THE WEDDING Maggie Sansone	Irish Traditions	IF YOU LOVE ME POLKA Various	Polish 25 Million Seller Hits Vol. 3
DAME TU AMORE GUANTANAMERA Yakare	Latin Cuban Jazz Salsa	MALA FEMMENA Al Ciaola	Italian Oro Italiano
DID YOUR MOTHER COME FROM IRELAND Bing Crosby	Irish Top O' the Morning	MEXICAN HAT DANCE Erich Kunzel	Latin Fiesta!
DODI LI Various	Jewish Klezmers Greatest Hits	MY WILD IRISH ROSE The Irish Tenors	Irish Ellis Island

♫ *Lyrics Provided*

ETHNIC DANCES

SONGS FOR ETHNIC DANCES

TITLE COMPOSER/ARTIST	GENRE/STYLE ALBUM	NOTES:
NEOPOLITAN SONG Bruna Bertone	Italian La Musica from Italy	
OSE SHALOM David & the High Spirits	Jewish To Life	
O SOLE MIO Roberto Alagna	Italian-Classical Roberto Alagna-Serenades	
RAISINS AND ALMONDS Mandy Patinkin	Jewish Mamaloshen	
SABBATH PRAYER Uri Cain	Jewish Knitting on the Roof	
TARANTELLA Various	Italian Italia Mia Vol.1	
TO LIFE Original Broadway Cast	Jewish Fiddler on the Roof	
TZENA TZENA The Barry Sisters	Jewish Their Greatest Yiddish Hits	
WHEN IRISH EYES ARE SMILING Bing Crosby	Irish Top 'O the Morning	
ZORBA THE GREEK Various	Greek Songs of Greece	

♫ *Lyrics Provided*

THE LAST DANCE

SELECTING SONGS FOR THE LAST DANCE

Before making your exit and starting your new life together, you and you new spouse may want to have a Last Dance. This is the perfect time to get one more romantic moment in, especially if you have been dancing with other friends and family throughout the reception.

If you and your spouse had trouble agreeing on a First Dance song, you may want to have one song played for the First Dance and one for the Last Dance. Once again, this is a chance to celebrate your love, so choose a song that has special meaning to you and your fiancé. You may want to start the last dance with just you and your new spouse and then have your DJ or bandleader invite everyone to join you.

SONGS FOR THE LAST DANCE

TITLE COMPOSER/ARTIST	GENRE/STYLE ALBUM	TITLE COMPOSER/ARTIST	GENRE/STYLE ALBUM
♫ A LITTLE MORE TIME ON YOU Alabama featuring N' Sync	Country Twentieth Century	♫ DREAM WEAVER Gary Wright	Rock Dream Weaver
♫ ALL I EVER NEED IS YOU Ray Charles	Country Complete Country...	GOODNIGHT SWEETHEART David Kersh	Country Goodnight Sweetheart
♫ ALL THROUGH THE NIGHT Cyndi Lauper	Pop All Through the Night	GOODNIGHT SWEETHEART The Flamingos	Motown The Best of the Flamingos
THE DANCE Garth Brooks	Country Garth Brooks	♫ I CROSS MY HEART George Strait	Country Pure Country
♫ DEDICATED TO THE ONE I LOVE Mamas & The Papas	Classic Pop Greatest Hits	♫ (I Love You) FOR SENTIMENTAL REASONS Ella Fitzgerald	Jazz Ella & Friends
DON'T SAY GOODNIGHT Isley Brothers	R&B Beautiful Ballads	(I've Had) THE TIME OF MY LIFE Bill Medley, Jennifer Warren	Pop Dirty Dancing
♫ DREAMING MY DREAMS WITH YOU Collin Raye	Country Love Songs	JUST TO SEE HER Smokey Robinson	R&B Ultimate Collection

♫ *Lyrics Provided*

THE LAST DANCE

SONGS FOR THE LAST DANCE

| TITLE | GENRE/STYLE |
COMPOSER/ARTIST	ALBUM
LAST DANCE	R&B
Donna Summer	Greatest Hits
♫ LOVE WILL FIND A WAY	Rock
Pablo Cruise	Worlds Away
♫ ON THE WINGS OF LOVE	R&B
Jeffrey Osborne	Love Songs
♫ ONE IN A MILLION YOU	R&B
Larry Graham	The Best of Larry Graham
SAVE THE BEST FOR LAST	R&B
Vanessa Williams	Greatest Hits…
♫ SHE BELIEVES IN ME	Country
Kenny Rogers	Love Collection
♫ YOU'RE STILL THE ONE	Country
Shania Twain	Come On Over
♫ THE VOWS GO UNBROKEN	County
Kenny Rogers	Decade of Hits

NOTES:

♫ *Lyrics Provided*

GENERAL

TIPS ON SELECTING SONGS FOR YOUR RECEPTION

It may seem like you have covered all the bases by choosing songs for all the special moments throughout your reception, but you also have to consider what will be played during the rest of the party. There are many factors to keep in mind while choosing the play list for your reception: how formal your wedding is, whether you have a band or a DJ, the location of the reception and your guests.

While you should feel free to choose music that you and your spouse enjoy, you will find that your guests will enjoy your reception more if you play a variety of musical genres. Play pieces from different eras- like swing, big band, Motown and 80's rock. If you are having a very formal reception you may want to stay with a musical theme, such as jazz standards or waltzes. For less formal receptions, get your guests up and dancing with party favorites like the Chicken Dance, the Bunny Hop, a Conga line and the Macarena.

Try to keep in mind that older guests, parents and children may not appreciate lyrics that can be considered offensive. Some church and temple halls will not allow certain music to be played even at the reception, so be sure to check and then pass along any restrictions to your DJ or band leader.

CAN'T MISS PARTY SONGS

TITLE	GENRE/STYLE	TITLE	GENRE/STYLE
COMPOSER/ARTIST	ALBUM	COMPOSER/ARTIST	ALBUM
ALLEY CAT	Big Band	THE HOKEY POKEY	Polka
Various Artists	Jukebox Party Classics	Brave Combo	Group Dance Epidemic
BORN TO HAND JIVE	Musical	HOT, HOT, HOT	Island Music
Original Broadway Cast	Grease	Buster Poindexter	Buster Poindexter
THE BUNNY HOP	Big Band	THE HUSTLE	Disco
Brave Combo	Group Dance Epidemic	Various	Pure Disco 2
CELEBRATION	Disco	ICE, ICE, BABY	Rap
Kool & the Gang	Celebration, Best Of	Vanilla Ice	Let It Rock 1990
THE CHICKEN DANCE	Polka	MACARENA	Spanish
Brave Combo	Group Dance Epidemic	Los Del Rio	Macarena Non Stop
ELECTRIC BOOGIE	Dance	TEQUILA	Oldies
Marcia Griffiths	Carousel	The Champs	Best Of

♫ *Lyrics Provided*

CAN'T MISS PARTY SONGS

TITLE	GENRE/STYLE
COMPOSER/ARTIST	ALBUM
THE TWIST	Oldies
Chubby Checker	Greatest Hits
THEME FROM	Oldies
NEW YORK, NEW YORK	In the Lounge
Mel Torme	With Mel Torme
STAYIN' ALIVE	Disco
Bee Gees	Saturday Night Fever, Soundtrack
YMCA	Disco
Village People	Pure Disco

NOTES:

♫ *Lyrics Provided*

GENERAL

NOTES:

MUSIC OPTIONS

DECIDING HOW YOU WANT YOUR MUSIC PLAYED DURING your ceremony and reception is just as important as choosing the right type of music. Your options are just as varied as the music itself. In this chapter, we will describe the different types of music providers and examine the advantages and disadvantages of each of the following options.

MUSIC PROVIDERS:

- Soloists
- Vocalists
- Trios and Quartets
- Chamber Ensembles
- Live Bands
- DJ
- Recorded Music

SOLOISTS

A soloist is a single musician performing live music. Typically, you would hire a wedding soloist that plays one of the following instruments:

- Harp
- Piano
- Guitar
- Flute
- Organ

Soloists most often perform as part of the wedding ceremony and may also be used to provide background music for the cocktail hour or beginning of the reception.

Things to Consider: Be sure that the soloist can perform your musical choices. Many classical pieces and some popular songs were written for specific instruments.

You will need to check on the availability of sheet music before deciding on a soloist. Also, you might want to ask your soloist to perform the specific piece you are most interested in before hiring him or her.

Price Range: Soloists are hired by the hour and typically charge $50 to $400 an hour.

VOCALISTS

Couples who want special hymns or songs to be performed during their ceremony often hire a vocalist. A vocalist is a singer that can perform songs either with or without musical accompaniment. You will need to be sure that the vocalist you choose can perform the songs that you want- often songs are written in specific pitches for a certain type of singer (i.e., soprano or tenor). Be sure to listen to your vocalist sing the exact song you want before signing any contracts.

MUSIC OPTIONS

Things to Consider: Be sure that any songs you might choose are appropriate for your ceremony site. Also, check with your ceremony site's wedding coordinator to see if he or she has any recommendations. Many churches have choir members who might be perfectly suited to perform at your wedding.

Price Ranges: Vocalists typically charge by the hour and can range from $50 per hour to $400 per hour.

TRIOS AND QUARTETS

Another popular choice for ceremony music is to hire a trio or quartet. This is a small group of musicians, three in a trio and four in a quartet, performing with instruments from the same family, or ones that compliment each other. Choices may include guitar trios, string quartets (featuring a violin, viola, and cello) or a combination of stringed instruments and flutes. Because trios and quartets have more instruments, there is a fuller sound to their performances and their repertoire is more extensive then a soloist's might be.

Things to Consider: Be sure to listen to the musicians as a group before hiring them, and be sure that the musicians you audition are the same ones who will perform at your wedding. Also, check that the group can perform your musical selection. Many classical pieces, as well as popular songs, have been arranged for performance by trios and quartets, so check on the availability of sheet music before deciding on a group.

Price Ranges: Trios and quartets often set prices based on the number of people in the group and range from $50 to $500 per hour, per person.

CHAMBER ENSEMBLES

Chamber ensembles are groups of classical musicians that perform a specific type of classical music. Chamber music is classical music written to be played in a small room or venue as opposed to a large symphony concert hall. This makes for a perfect choice for many wedding ceremonies, as well as the cocktail and dinner hours of your reception. The music available for chamber ensembles is varied, including pieces written just for chamber musicians, as well as pieces originally written for larger orchestras that have been arranged for the smaller ensemble.

Things to Consider: Chamber ensembles often only play classical pieces and may not have experience with instrumental versions of popular songs. So if you have chosen "Wind Beneath My Wings" as the song that will be playing while your mother takes her seat, a chamber ensemble may not be a good choice. Also, if there will be dancing at your reception, a chamber ensemble will not be appropriate, so you may have to hire different musicians for your reception.

Price Ranges: The cost for chamber ensembles are usually set based on the number of people in the group, and range from $50 to $500 per hour, per person.

LIVE BAND

Many couples hire live bands to perform at their weddings. A live band can be as small as four musicians playing the guitar, drums, piano and bass, to a full Big Band complete with a horn section. Bands go a long way in creating an atmosphere for a wedding, especially at the reception. Hiring a band that will play all jazz numbers helps to make your wedding completely different than a wedding that has all Big Band music. A band playing dance standards from the Forties and Fifties also creates a more formal feel to your wedding. You might want to consider hiring a local rock band, maybe one that you and your fiancé saw perform on one of your early dates. A good live band will keep your guests on their feet and having fun throughout your reception.

Things to Consider: The cost goes up with the number of musicians in the band so you may want to look for smaller groups. Also, it is harder to control the volume of a large live band, so check with your reception site to see how late loud music can be played. Consider if you want loud music at all. If you have many older guests or want your guests to be able to spend time talking to one another, a live rock band may not be the best choice.

Price Ranges: Live bands are hired on an hourly or per event and can run from $400 to $5,000.

DJ

A DJ is a popular choice for providing music at many weddings. A DJ will provide an extensive library of recorded music to play throughout your wedding. With a DJ, you have many more options for music throughout your ceremony and reception than you do when you hire musicians. A good DJ will have recordings of everything from classical music for your ceremony, to the most popular first dance songs, to all-time party favorites. With a DJ, you also have more control over volume and can choose any music that you can find already recorded. A DJ can also ensure that your party flows smoothly by watching the reactions of your guests to certain music. In this way, your DJ can change the play list to reflect what people like throughout the party.

Things to Consider: When looking at a DJ's song list, make sure that the music is varied from different genres and eras. If you are having your ceremony and reception at a religious site, be sure to let your DJ know what can and cannot be played.

Price Ranges: DJs charge by the hour and typically you must hire them for a minimum number of hours. The hourly rate ranges from $50 to $300, with a typical commitment of two to five hours.

MUSIC OPTIONS

RECORDED MUSIC

Some couples choose to use recorded music without hiring a DJ. This is most often possible during the ceremony when you can use your ceremony site's wedding coordinator or a close friend to queue up specific songs. If you are choosing music that is already in your personal music collection, this can be a big money saver. It will require you to put together a list of what is to be played and when during the ceremony. It will also require that whomever you put in charge of the music understands exactly what you want. Be sure that the person who will be playing the music is present at the rehearsal and use that time to run through your musical selections as well.

Things to Consider: Using recorded music that someone plays over a sound system works best if you can "burn" a CD of the music you want in the order you want it. Also, be sure that all the music is appropriate for your ceremony site, is the correct length, and that your ceremony site has an adequate sound system that you can use.

Price Ranges: From $5 to $50, depending on whether or not you need to purchase recordings of songs you want.

HIRING A MUSIC PROFESSIONAL

ONCE YOU DECIDE WHAT MUSIC you want and how you want the music played - either live or recorded, by a soloist or a full band - you need to find the right musicians or DJ. In this chapter we will discuss:

- **How to choose a Soloist or Vocalist**

- **How to choose a Trio, Quartet or Ensemble**

- **How to choose a Band**

- **How to choose a DJ**

- **What questions to ask**

- **What to look for in a music professional**

- **What to avoid**

HOW TO CHOOSE A SOLOIST OR VOCALIST

When choosing a soloist or vocalist to perform at your wedding, there are a few things to consider: When and for how long do you want them to perform? Do you need them for the entire ceremony? Do you want them to perform during the cocktail and dinner hours of your reception? The longer you need a vocalist or soloist to perform, the more music they need to have in their repertoire. A flutist who only performs during the interlude and postlude will not have to have as varied a song list as one who needs to perform during the processional and recessional as well. Also, consider the songs you have chosen for the different parts of your ceremony and ask yourself how they will sound when performed by a single person or instrument. Ask the vocalist or soloist to provide you with a demo tape containing performances of typical wedding music they have recently performed. Also, ask them if it is possible for an in-person audition. This is especially important if your musical choices are unusual. In that case, you will want to hear him/her perform your specific songs. Be prepared to pay a small fee if your vocalist or soloist does not usually provide auditions.

HOW TO CHOOSE A TRIO, QUARTET OR ENSEMBLE

Before choosing a Trio, Quartet or Ensemble, you must again ask yourself some questions. How long do you want them to play? What types of music are you interested in having at your ceremony? Do you want the musicians to perform during your reception? If you have a song list for your ceremony that includes both classical pieces and instrumental versions of popular songs, you will want to check to make sure that the musicians are familiar with your popular song selections. If your musicians can provide a demo recording, be sure to ask if the same musicians featured on the recording are the ones who will be performing at your wedding. If you have unusual or unique song selections, ask your musicians to audition performing one of your selections. If an in-person audition is not something that the musicians typically offer, you may have to pay a small fee.

HOW TO CHOOSE A BAND

There are as many types of bands as there are types of music, so narrowing down your search can be a little difficult. Begin by deciding when you want the band to play. Will they need to provide music for the ceremony or just the reception? Next, consider the size of your reception venue. A large band will overwhelm a small room, while a small band may not have enough volume to engage everyone in a larger setting. Finally, consider what types of music you are most interested in. A jazz band may not be familiar with today's pop hits, while a band that plays traditional wedding favorites may not perform a unique, personal favorite up to your standards. Also, be sure to inquire about equipment needs. A band that has a lot of equipment and needs multiple electrical outlets may have a problem performing outdoors.

HOW TO CHOOSE A DJ

A great DJ can make a party, just as a not so great one can ruin it, so it is important that you choose carefully. If you open up your phone book to "DJ", you will find an almost endless list of people available in your area. The key to finding a good DJ is to find an experienced professional with an extensive song list. While DJs don't have demo tapes, many will provide a video that will give you an idea of their style. Along with the DJ's personal style, you will want to evaluate their play list. Look for a wide variety of music, from different genres, as well as different eras. Inquire into the DJ's level of commitment; is the DJ doing this to earn extra money on the weekends or are weddings the DJ's primary business? A higher level of commitment often means a higher level of professionalism as the DJ relies on referrals.

The DJ often acts as the reception's Master of Ceremony (MC). So look for someone who has a great voice as well as the ability to move things along smoothly.

HIRING A MUSIC PROFESSIONAL

WHAT QUESTIONS TO ASK

The best way to compare any of your music professionals is to ask them a series of questions. You will be able to get the information you need to make an informed choice and help to prevent a musical mishap on your big day. Below is a list of questions and explanations of things to look for when hiring a professional. After the questions you will find worksheets that you can use to compare your choices.

What are the particulars?

Start by getting the exact name of the band or DJ service, their address and phone number. If you find someone who is perfect, you want to be sure you can get ahold of him or her again. Also, having the exact name will make checking into their references much easier.

How many years of professional experience do you have?

Experience goes a long way in the professional music business. Professionals who have been performing at weddings for a long period of time are more likely to have seen it all and will stay calm and collected should anything not go according to plan. Professional experience also provides a track record for you to check into.

What percentage of your business is dedicated to weddings?

Many musicians moonlight in addition to their day jobs, and so they may not have performed at many weddings. Performing for a wedding is different from performing in a professional orchestra, being a high school band teacher, or even performing at other types of functions. You want your music professional to specialize in weddings as much as possible.

Are you the person who will be performing at my wedding?

Make sure that the people you interview, listen to demo tapes from or personally audition are the same people who will be performing at your wedding. Of course emergencies sometimes arise, but you want to be sure that the wedding performance will be of the same caliber as the audition. The best way to ensure this is by having the same music professionals.

What instruments do you play?

Make sure that any musician you are interested in hiring plays the instrument you are most interested in. Many musicians play multiple instruments, but specialize in one particular type, so check to make sure that the instrument you will want him or her to play is the one he or she is the most proficient with.

What type of music do you specialize in?

If you have a specific theme or atmosphere you are hoping to create at your wedding, this question is especially important. You want your DJ or musicians to specialize in the music you are most interested in. Hiring a band that does 80's cover tunes to perform jazz standards is a recipe for disaster.

HIRING A MUSIC PROFESSIONAL

WHAT QUESTIONS TO ASK (CONT'D)

What are your hourly fees?
Ask this question during your initial contact with any music professional for comparisons, but ask for the quote in writing when you are narrowing down your search. You don't want your other musician choices to book up while you are trying to make a decision only to find that the remaining ones have raised their prices.

Do you have an hourly minimum requirement?
Since most wedding ceremony and receptions last for many hours, minimums may not matter. However, if you are hiring a musician to perform only at your ceremony, you may want to be sure that the hourly minimum requirement will not run much longer than your ceremony. Some ceremonies are as short as thirty minutes, so if your musician has a two-hour minimum, you may be paying them for time they are not actually performing.

What is the cost of a soloist/duet/trio/quartet?
Some musicians will be able to work within your budget by changing the number of musicians they perform with.

What is your cost for additional hours?
If your reception is in full swing, or if your ceremony starts a little later than originally planned, you want to be sure your musicians will be able to stay for the duration. You will also want to establish the cost for additional time BEFORE the situation arises.

How will you dress for my wedding?
You want your music professionals to come to your wedding properly attired. That can mean tuxedos and formal dresses, Zoot suits from the 1940's, or Renaissance inspired costumes. If your wedding has a theme, check to see if the musicians are willing to dress accordingly. Be prepared to pay the costs of costume rental if you are asking for something unusual.

Do you have a cordless microphone?
When it is time for toasts at the reception, you will want to have a cordless microphone. This will allow the person giving the toast to stand in front of your guests without having to go on stage. Most band leaders or DJs will allow you to use their cordless microphone, but be sure to check that they have one and that you can use it during the reception.

What equipment will you bring? Do you have back-up equipment/musicians?
Check to make sure that any music professional you are interested in hiring has all his/her own equipment, including items such as extension cords and power strips. Also, ensure that your music professional will have back-up equipment to use if there are any equipment failures. Equally important are back-up professionals. If the DJ, or someone in the band, is ill or has an emergency, who will come in their place?

WHAT QUESTIONS TO ASK (CONT'D)

How many breaks will you take and for how long?
Your music professional will need to take a few breaks sometime during your wedding. Just be sure they are not expecting an excessive amount of break time.

Will you play recorded music during your break?
Your DJ can easily play recorded music during any breaks, but you want to be sure that any musicians you hire can do the same. Be sure that they have the equipment to play recorded music, and ask if you need to provide the recorded music or if they will bring it with them.

Who is responsible for the musicians' food and where will they eat?
Often, music professionals expect to be served the same meal that your guests will be eating. You will need to include them in your guest count if this is the case, so take that into consideration. If you prefer, you may be able to make arrangements to serve them a simpler meal, such as sandwiches or hamburgers. Also, decide beforehand where you want your musicians to eat.

Do you have liability insurance?
Some musicians will require a bride and groom to sign a contract that will make them responsible for any damage done to their equipment during the wedding. Because this leaves the bride and groom open to the possibility of having to pay large sums in damages, or even to lawsuits, you may want to make sure that the music professional you are interested in hiring carries his or her own insurance. Check to see what the insurance will cover as well, since you may want to augment it with your own wedding insurance.

What is your payment/cancellation policy?
Payment and cancellation policies vary so find one that meets your needs. You may also want to ask your music professionals if they can work within your budget. Perhaps they could take a larger down payment, but give you longer time to pay the balance due.

HIRING A MUSIC PROFESSIONAL

NOTES:

Comparison Chart
For Hiring Music
Professionals

THE FOLLOWING COMPARISON CHARTS ARE PROVIDED for you to use when selecting your music professionals. Asking a variety of questions will help you best determine the most suitable professional for your wedding.

MUSIC PROFESSIONAL COMPARISON CHART

QUESTIONS	POSSIBILITY 1	POSSIBILITY 2
What is the name of the DJ, Musician, or Band?		
What is the contact person's name and phone number?		
What is your address?		
How many years of professional experience do you have?		
What percentage of your business is dedicated to weddings?		
Are you the person who will be performing at my wedding?		
What instruments do you play?		
What type of music do you specialize in?		
What are your hourly fees?		
Do you have an hourly minimum?		
What is your cost for a four-hour reception?		
What is your cost for each additional hour?		
How will you dress for my wedding?		
Do you have a cordless microphone?		
What equipment will you bring?		
Do you have back-up equipment?		
Do you have back-up musicians/DJs?		
How many breaks will you take and for how long?		

MUSIC PROFESSIONAL COMPARISON CHART

POSSIBILITY 3	POSSIBILITY 4	POSSIBILITY 5	POSSIBILITY 6

MUSIC PROFESSIONAL COMPARISON CHART

QUESTIONS	POSSIBILITY 1	POSSIBILITY 2
Will you play recorded music during your break?		
Who is responsible for the musician's/DJ's food?		
Where do the musician/DJs expect to eat?		
Do you have liability insurance?		
What is your payment/cancellation policy?		
Other:		
Other:		
Other:		
Other:		
Other:		
Other:		
Other:		
Other:		
Other:		
Other:		
Other:		
Other:		
Other:		

MUSIC PROFESSIONAL COMPARISON CHART

POSSIBILITY 3	POSSIBILITY 4	POSSIBILITY 5	POSSIBILITY 6

MUSIC PROFESSIONAL COMPARISON CHART

NOTES:

SIGNING
THE CONTRACT

ONCE YOU HAVE DECIDED WHAT MUSIC PROFESSIONALS to hire for your wedding, you will need to sign a contract. Many music professionals have standard contracts that they use as part of their business, but almost all contracts cover the same material. Before signing a contract, you should review the following information and become familiar with such issues as how to negotiate the best deal, key points of a standard contract, traps to avoid, etc.

HOW TO NEGOTIATE
THE BEST DEAL

Because music plays such an important part in your wedding, it can be expensive. There are ways, however, to negotiate a better deal and to save money. Begin by establishing your budget for music, and stick to it. Explain to each music professional that you are interested in hiring within your budget and ask them what they can provide within that budget. Because you need music for both the ceremony and the reception, see if musicians or DJs will offer you a better deal if you hire them for both parts of the wedding. If you are approaching a musician, ask if you can hire him/her as a soloist, or perhaps hire a duet for the ceremony at a price break if you hire the entire band for the reception. Approach a DJ with the same idea. Begin by telling the DJ that you are considering a soloist or trio, for example, for your ceremony

and a DJ for the reception. Then ask if the DJ would be willing to give you a price break to play recordings of the ceremony music you have chosen (instead of hiring the soloist or trio) if you hire him or her for the reception as well.

TRAPS TO AVOID

Most music professionals in the wedding business are honest, hard-working people who take great pride in providing you with a high quality service that will enhance your special day. Unfortunately, there are a few unscrupulous people in every profession, and you want to be sure you do not inadvertently hire one for your wedding. Here is a brief list of things to check to make sure that you are hiring a true professional. Of course, this doesn't guarantee that the musician is honest, but it will serve as a good way to begin the interview process.

SIGNING THE CONTRACT

Traps to Avoid Checklist

- ❑ Check with the Better Business Bureau in your area. Do they have any complaints on file?
- ❑ Can the music professional give you the names and numbers of their three most recent customers so you can call to get references?
- ❑ Can the music professional provide you with three professional references?
- ❑ Does the music professional use a contract?

KEY POINTS IN A STANDARD CONTRACT

Make sure that everything you have agreed to with your music professional is guaranteed, in writing, in the contract. This serves to protect you as well as the music professional and will go a long way in making sure that the music for your wedding is perfect. The following are key points that should be covered in any contract.

Contract Checklist

- ❑ The date, time and location of the wedding.
- ❑ The exact time that the music professional will start and end.
- ❑ The hourly rate of the music professional, the minimum required time and the hourly rate for any additional time that might become necessary.
- ❑ The name of the DJ, or each musician who will perform. Clearly state who will be performing in case of illness or emergency cancellation - and how to get a hold of that person.
- ❑ A list of all equipment the band or DJ will bring. Be sure it is spelled out if you have agreed to bring anything as well.
- ❑ A description of the DJ's or Emcee's duties - including any pre-wedding meetings to go over your musical program.
- ❑ The number and duration of breaks, and if recorded music will be played during those breaks.
- ❑ A description of what the DJ or band will be wearing (appropriate, acceptable attire).
- ❑ A list of special songs to be played. If you have asked the band to learn new songs be sure you specify that they will be rehearsed prior to the wedding.
- ❑ A clear description of the payment and cancellation policy.
- ❑ A statement that the bride or groom will not be held responsible for damages done to equipment by guests or any other third party.

WEDDING MUSIC TIMELINE

BECAUSE MUSIC IS SUCH AN ESSENTIAL PART OF YOUR WEDDING, it is important to set up a planning timeline. Following this timeline will allow you to pick the best music professionals at the best prices, rather than being forced to make last minute decisions you will later regret. This timeline assumes that you have 9-12 months to plan your wedding, but it can be adjusted to fit your schedule.

WEDDING MUSIC TIMELINE

NINE MONTHS TO ONE YEAR BEFORE THE WEDDING

- ❏ Book the location of your ceremony and reception
- ❏ Decide on types of music (classical, popular, jazz, etc.)
- ❏ Begin filling in the Comparison Chart for Hiring Music Professionals found on page 58.

SIX TO NINE MONTHS BEFORE THE WEDDING

- ❏ Make a final decision on your music professional
- ❏ Carefully review and sign music professional contract
- ❏ Begin filling in the Music Selections and Preferences worksheets

THREE TO FOUR MONTHS BEFORE THE WEDDING

- ❏ Make final decisions on music choices for special dances, Recessional and Processional, Unity Candle, etc.
- ❏ Purchase any needed sheet music or CDs (be sure to give yourself enough time to special order items if needed)
- ❏ Write out a script and schedule of announcements you want your DJ or Emcee to make (see Script/Announcements for DJ/Emcee worksheet on page 82.)

FOUR TO SIX WEEKS BEFORE THE WEDDING

- ❏ Meet with music professional and go over your final selections and special requests/instructions
- ❏ Re-confirm all details of the music for the wedding, including address of ceremony and reception, final payment, and music choices
- ❏ Give sheet music or CDs to music professional

ONE WEEK BEFORE THE WEDDING

- ❏ Make a final phone call to music professional to confirm all details
- ❏ Give music professional's tip to your wedding coordinator, Maid of Honor, or Best Man (whomever will be in charge of tipping at your reception)
- ❏ Make any final payments as specified in your contract

CREATING YOUR MUSIC STYLE

YOUR WEDDING SHOULD BE A REFLECTION of you and your fiancé's personalities. Choosing a style for your wedding is the first step to making your special day a reality. Once you have decided on the style, your musical selections will fall into place.

Remember that there are many other people to consider in your wedding planning, and you should ask for as much input in the musical selection as you are comfortable with. This is especially true if you have parents or other relatives who are helping to pay for your wedding.

Use the worksheets on the following pages to help narrow down your musical choices, and to help make sure that your music will create the sense of style you are looking for in your special day.

SELECTIONS AND PREFERENCES

PART OF THE WEDDING	SONGS THE BRIDE LIKES	SONGS THE GROOM LIKES
Prelude		
Pre-Processional		
Processional		
Bride's Entrance		
Ceremony Song 1		
Ceremony Song 2		
Unity Candle Lighting		
Reciting the Vows		
Recessional		
Interlude		
Cocktails		
Dinner/Meal		
Newlywed's Entrance		
First Dance		
Father/Daughter Dance		
Mother/Son Dance		
Other Family Dance		
Cake Cutting		

SELECTIONS AND PREFERENCES

SONGS THE BRIDE'S FAMILY LIKES	SONGS THE GROOM'S FAMILY LIKES	PROFESSIONAL RECOMMENDATIONS

SELECTIONS AND PREFERENCES

PART OF THE WEDDING	SONGS THE BRIDE LIKES	SONGS THE GROOM LIKES
Garter Removal/Toss		
Bouquet Toss		
Last Dance		
Other:		
Other:		
Other:		
Other:		
Other:		
Other:		
Other:		
Other:		
Other:		
Other:		
Other:		
Other:		
Other:		
Other:		

SELECTIONS AND PREFERENCES

SONGS THE BRIDE'S FAMILY LIKES	SONGS THE GROOM'S FAMILY LIKES	PROFESSIONAL RECOMMENDATIONS

FINAL SELECTIONS

MAKING YOUR FINAL SELECTIONS

Once you have narrowed down your choices to three, fill in these charts and have the bride (B), the groom (G), the bride's family (BF), and the groom's family (GF) vote on one for each section.

FINAL SELECTION SONG CHART

• PRELUDE

SONG	B Vote	G Vote	BF Vote	GF Vote

• PRE-PROCESSIONAL

SONG	B Vote	G Vote	BF Vote	GF Vote

• PROCESSIONAL

SONG	B Vote	G Vote	BF Vote	GF Vote

• BRIDAL ENTRANCE

SONG	B Vote	G Vote	BF Vote	GF Vote

• CEREMONY SONG 1

SONG	B Vote	G Vote	BF Vote	GF Vote

• CEREMONY SONG 2

SONG	B Vote	G Vote	BF Vote	GF Vote

• VOWS

SONG	B Vote	G Vote	BF Vote	GF Vote

• UNITY CANDLE

SONG	B Vote	G Vote	BF Vote	GF Vote

• RECESSIONAL

SONG	B Vote	G Vote	BF Vote	GF Vote

FINAL SELECTIONS

• COCKTAILS

SONG	B Vote	G Vote	BF Vote	GF Vote

• DINNER/MEAL

SONG	B Vote	G Vote	BF Vote	GF Vote

• NEWLYWED ENTRANCE

SONG	B Vote	G Vote	BF Vote	GF Vote

• FIRST DANCE

SONG	B Vote	G Vote	BF Vote	GF Vote

• FATHER/DAUGHTER DANCE

SONG	B Vote	G Vote	BF Vote	GF Vote

• MOTHER/SON DANCE

SONG	B Vote	G Vote	BF Vote	GF Vote

• OTHER FAMILY DANCES

SONG	B Vote	G Vote	BF Vote	GF Vote

• CAKE CUTTING

SONG	B Vote	G Vote	BF Vote	GF Vote

• GARTER-TOSS

SONG	B Vote	G Vote	BF Vote	GF Vote

• BOUQUET TOSS

SONG	B Vote	G Vote	BF Vote	GF Vote

FINAL SELECTIONS

• LAST DANCE

SONG	B Vote	G Vote	BF Vote	GF Vote

• OTHER:

SONG	B Vote	G Vote	BF Vote	GF Vote

NOTES:

WRITING A MUSIC PROGRAM

IT IS IMPORTANT TO WRITE A PROGRAM for both your ceremony and reception to share with your music professional. In the program, clearly indicate which songs you want played/performed for each part of the ceremony, the approximate time you expect the music to begin, and if you are having an Emcee or DJ host the reception, what you want announced before each part. Providing a program will ensure that everything runs smoothly and that the perfect song is playing for every moment of your wedding.

In this chapter, you will find worksheets that you can use to cover every aspect of your ceremony and reception. If you choose not to include certain dances or moments in your wedding, simply write "Not Applicable" (N/A) in those boxes. Make copies and provide one for each of your music professionals, as well as your wedding coordinator if you have hired one. You should also have a copy with your belongings the day of the wedding in case a replacement musician or DJ is sent who is not familiar with your musical program.

MUSIC PROGRAM

CEREMONY MUSIC PROGRAM

The Wedding Of: Date: Time:

Location of Ceremony:

Address:

City: State: Zip Code:

Phone Number:

Contact Person for Ceremony Site:

Set Up Time:

Set Up Location:

PART OF THE CEREMONY	SONG	ARTIST	CUE (when music professional will begin playing/ performing selection)
PRELUDE			
PRELUDE			
PRELUDE			
PRELUDE			
PRE-PROCESSIONAL			
PROCESSIONAL			
BRIDE'S ENTRANCE			
CEREMONY SONG			
CEREMONY SONG			

MUSIC PROGRAM

CEREMONY MUSIC PROGRAM

PART OF THE CEREMONY	SONG	ARTIST	CUE *(when music professional will begin playing/ performing selection)*
UNITY CANDLE			
RECITING THE VOWS			
RECESSIONAL			
INTERLUDE/POSTLUDE			
INTERLUDE/POSTLUDE			
INTERLUDE/POSTLUDE			
OTHER			
OTHER			
OTHER			
OTHER			
OTHER			
OTHER			
OTHER			
OTHER			
OTHER			

MUSIC PROGRAM

RECEPTION MUSIC PROGRAM

The Wedding Of: Date: Time:

Location of Reception:

Address:

City: State: Zip Code:

Phone Number:

Contact Person for Reception Site:

Set Up Time:

Set Up Location:

PART OF THE RECEPTION	SONG	ARTIST	CUE (when music professional will begin playing/ performing selection)
COCKTAILS			
COCKTAILS			
NEWLYWED ENTRANCE			
DINNER/MEAL			
DINNER/MEAL			
DINNER/MEAL			
FIRST DANCE			
FATHER-DAUGHTER DANCE			
MOTHER-SON DANCE			

MUSIC PROGRAM

RECEPTION MUSIC PROGRAM

PART OF THE RECEPTION	SONG	ARTIST	CUE *(when music professional will begin playing/ performing selection)*
OTHER FAMILY DANCES			
CAKE CUTTING			
GARTER-TOSS			
BOUQUET-TOSS			
MONEY DANCE			
LAST DANCE			
OTHER			
OTHER			
OTHER			
OTHER			
OTHER			
OTHER			
OTHER			
OTHER			
OTHER			

MUSIC PROGRAM

SCRIPT/ANNOUNCEMENTS FOR DJ/EMCEE

Bridal Entrance:

First Dance:

Father/Daughter Dance:

Mother/Son Dance:

Other Family Dance:

Cake-Cutting:

MUSIC PROGRAM

SCRIPT/ANNOUNCEMENTS FOR DJ/EMCEE

Garter-Toss:

Bouquet-Toss:

Money Dance:

Last Dance:

Other:

Other:

MUSIC PROGRAM

WEDDING PARTY:

ROLE IN WEDDING	NAME
Bride:	
Groom:	
Mother of Bride:	
Father of Bride:	
Mother of Groom:	
Father of Groom:	
Best Man:	
Maid/Matron of Honor:	
Usher/Groomsman:	
Usher/Groomsman:	
Usher/Groomsman:	
Usher/Groomsman:	
Usher/Groomsman:	
Usher/Groomsman:	
Bridesmaid:	
Bridesmaid:	
Bridesmaid:	
Bridesmaid:	
Bridesmaid:	
Bridesmaid:	
Flower Girl:	
Ring Bearer:	
Grandparents of Bride:	
Grandparents of Groom:	
Other_____:	
Other_____:	

MUSIC CHECKLISTS

WITH EVERYTHING THAT NEEDS TO BE DONE while planning a wedding, there can be many small details that fall by the wayside. Be sure to check and double check all of your contracts, worksheets, comparison charts and any other forms that you have completed in the previous sections to make sure you have everything taken care of. The following are two checklists to help remind you of the tasks that need to be completed for your wedding music.

EQUIPMENT CHECKLIST

This is a list of equipment commonly used by music professionals. Use this checklist to determine who is responsible for providing what for the wedding. You may also choose to make a copy of the checklist to share with your music professional, and perhaps attach a copy to any contract you sign.

THINGS TO DO CHECKLIST

This is a list of all of the items that need to be taken care of to finalize your ceremony and reception music. The checklist is based on the items that are included in the previous sections of the music guide. Once you have completed each section, you can mark the task as "Done." This will help you keep track of all your accomplishments.

MUSIC CHECKLISTS

EQUIPMENT CHECKLIST

EQUIPMENT		YOU WILL BRING	PROFESSIONAL WILL BRING
Chairs	Enter Qty:	❑	❑
Cordless Microphones	Enter Qty:	❑	❑
Extension Cords	Enter Qty:	❑	❑
Power Strips	Enter Qty:	❑	❑
Music Stands	Enter Qty:	❑	❑
Lights	Enter Qty:	❑	❑
Speakers	Enter Qty:	❑	❑
Monitor	Enter Qty:	❑	❑
PA System	Enter Qty:	❑	❑
Other:		❑	❑
Other:		❑	❑
Other:		❑	❑

THINGS TO DO CHECKLIST

DONE   TO ACCOMPLISH

- ❑ Complete Comparison Chart for Hiring Music Professionals for at least three possibilities
- ❑ Decide on musical style for ceremony
- ❑ Decide on musical style for reception
- ❑ Complete Song Selection and Preferences Chart
- ❑ Make final selection of music professionals
- ❑ Carefully review and sign music professional's contract
- ❑ Have your fiancé and family vote on final three selections
- ❑ Make final determination of songs for all parts of the ceremony and reception
- ❑ Purchase/order sheet music and/or recordings of special songs and give them to your music professional
- ❑ Write music program for ceremony and reception
- ❑ Meet with music professional to review and give them a copy of your music programs
- ❑ Give an envelope to the Best Man with final payment and tip for music professionals

A Crash Course in Classical Music

CLASSICAL MUSIC FOR YOUR WEDDING AND LIFE TOGETHER

By Rebecca Davis, Naxos of America, Manager of Publicity
and Promotions and Wedding Music Consultant

The process of choosing music for your impending nuptials can certainly be a daunting process. There are so many choices out there and the questions are endless. Do you want traditional wedding music or something off the beaten path? Will your mother cry if you don't march down the aisle to Wagner and back out again to Mendelssohn, or are you willing to try something new? This short primer is designed to give you some pointers to navigate the world of classical music for your wedding. It includes all of the standards, as well as some pieces that you may have heard before but never considered for a wedding, and some beautiful treasures that you may have never heard before but that will make your wedding a unique musical experience for everyone in attendance. The process can be exciting indeed as you choose your own unique soundtrack for your wedding day. Who knows? It may spark a desire to learn more about classical music for enjoyment in your married life together.

A CRASH COURSE IN CLASSICAL MUSIC

OPEN YOUR EARS

First things first...listen. What have you heard at other weddings that you've really liked? What about concerts, church services or even on radio, television or at the movies? You can find some beautiful musical choices from all of these sources if you just open your ears. In fact, most of the music most commonly used in weddings was originally written for something else entirely. For instance, Wagner's traditional "Here Comes the Bride" march was originally written for the tragic opera *Lohengrin*. Likewise, Mendelssohn's traditional recessional was written as incidental music for Shakespeare's play, *A Midsummer Night's Dream*.

DO YOUR RESEARCH

If you have the luxury of a good public library with music or a local university music library, those are great places to research music for your wedding. Ask the librarian to assist you with finding classical music that might be appropriate for a wedding or a good beginner's guide to classical music. Another great place to listen is at your local music retailer. Many music companies make your job easier by publishing wedding music CDs with traditional favorites included. Internet music retailers will usually have several of these with audio samples so that you can hear for yourself whether the piece might be something you'd like played either walking down the aisle, or while you and your groom light the Unity candle.

As soon as you find some pieces of music that you know you like, whether from the library, the internet, a concert or another wedding, jot down as much information about the piece as possible (usually this is on the track listing of the CD or the wedding program) and take it to your local music store or to your musicians. The most critical things to note are the composer and the title of the piece.

Don't forget to write down some of those Opus, BWV, or K numbers if they are listed - you won't regret it. Believe it or not, they serve a very important purpose. For example: If you tell your organist that you are interested in the Bach organ prelude you've been humming all day, he'll be lost among the hundreds of preludes Bach wrote unless you give him the number associated with the piece. Titles can vary widely, but the more information you give your musicians, the better your chances for getting the piece that you want. Think of it as a Dewey Decimal System for composers.

Here is how it works... Opus (which literally means "work") is the catch-all phrase used to list the work numbers of any given composers. The Opus numbers are given by the historians who catalogued the composer's music. The numbers are based on the period of life in which the piece was written. Any composer's Opus 1 will likely be his first work (or at least the first he'll admit to) and the highest Opus number will be the final work that he wrote.

For some of the most notable composers in history, such as Bach, Schubert, Vivaldi or Mozart, historians used their own names as a way to catalogue the composer's music. This is why you'll often see a K listing after Mozart's works. K is the abbreviation for Köchel, the musicologist who listed all of Mozart's works from a Piano Miniature K.1 written when he was just 5 to the Requiem K.626 written from his deathbed.

A CRASH COURSE IN CLASSICAL MUSIC

Likewise, you'll see the abbreviation BWV with J.S. Bach, D with Schubert and R with Vivaldi.

It's not as important to know the details about the origins of work numbers as long as you know that the numbers are an important part of identifying a certain piece. As with many of the esoteric elements of any art form, even the most educated don't always know what each term means, but the terms help keep the innumerable compositions manageable so that you can find the piece that you are most anxious to find. If all else fails, hum the tune; you're likely to find someone who knows what it is before long.

NAVIGATING THE CD BINS

Most classical music sections in your local music retailer are alphabetized by composer, with additional sections for operas, different genres (types of musical compositions like orchestral, choral, instrumental, etc) and varieties of music. Ask a staff member for suggestions of music for beginners. A good place to start is the Naxos A-Z of Classical Music, a 2 CD set with a 500 page music reference. In addition to beginner's guides and wedding music compilations, many record companies make it easy to enjoy the classics for life with collections designed for all manner of different activities: from exercising, to sleeping, to playing, to hosting a holiday party. These kinds of titles will help you get started on your journey into the fantastic world of classical music. Where you go from there only takes some curiosity and an ear for good music.

MUSIC FOR LIFE

With this information in hand, we hope you will be better prepared to find the perfect music for your special day, even if you've never worked with classical music before. We hope that your journey into the world of classical music will give you a new appreciation for the art form and realize that classical music can be an ideal accompaniment for all of your life, even beyond your wedding day. Consider classical music to accompany your studies, an elegant dinner party, to calm a child or to enjoy for its own sake. You will discover that there is a vast repertoire of music to discover from the past 400 years that can be enjoyed long after the vows have been said and the cake has been cut on your wedding day.

SUGGESTED LISTENING ON NAXOS:

- Discover the Classics 8.550035-36

- A-Z of Classical Music...8.55319-20

- Naxos Family Classics 8.555293, 8.555294, 8.555291, 8.55292

- Listen, Learn and Grow Playtime... 8.560050

- Ave Maria 8.553751

- Wedding Music 8.550790

- Dance of the Blessed Spirits...8.554166

- Classical Music Start-Up Kits...8.550779, 8.550835

MY POCKET WEDDING PLANNER

This handy pocket planner is included so you can keep all your important wedding planning information with you at all times. Tuck this little planner in your purse or pocket as an easy reference when you are on the go! This convenient booklet includes the following sections:

- Wedding Information at a Glance
    - Wedding Events at a Glance
    - Vendor Information at a Glance
- Wedding Planning Checklist
- Checklist of Budget Items
- Budget Analysis
- 12-Month Wedding Planning Calendar
- Wedding Planning Notes

This booklet is companion guide to a Wedding Solutions'
best-selling wedding planning book.
Not to be sold separately.

Cover Image: Karen French
Karen French Photography
8351 Elmcrest Lane
Huntington Beach, CA 92646
1-800-734-6219
info@karenfrenchphotography.com
www.karenfrenchphotography.com

Available nationally and internationally
Based in Orange County, California

WEDDING INFORMATION AT A GLANCE

WEDDING EVENTS AT A GLANCE

ENGAGEMENT PARTY DATE: Time:

Location:

Address:

Contact Person:

Phone Number:

Website:

E-mail:

BRIDAL SHOWER DATE: Time:

Location:

Address:

Contact Person:

Phone Number:

Website:

E-mail:

WEDDING EVENTS AT A GLANCE

BACHELOR PARTY DATE: Time:

Location:

Address:

Contact Person:

Phone Number:

Website:

E-mail:

BACHELORETTE PARTY DATE: Time:

Location:

Address:

Contact Person:

Phone Number:

Website:

E-mail:

CEREMONY REHEARSAL DATE: Time:

Location:

Address:

Contact Person:

Phone Number:

Website:

E-mail:

WEDDING EVENTS AT A GLANCE

REHEARSAL DINNER DATE: Time:

Location:

Address:

Contact Person:

Phone Number:

Website:

E-mail:

CEREMONY DATE: Time:

Location:

Address:

Contact Person:

Phone Number:

Website:

E-mail:

RECEPTION DATE: Time:

Location:

Address:

Contact Person:

Phone Number:

Website:

E-mail:

VENDOR INFORMATION AT A GLANCE

WEDDING CONSULTANT

Company:

Contact Person:

Phone Number:

Website:

E-mail:

CEREMONY SITE

Company:

Contact Person:

Phone Number:

Website:

E-mail:

RECEPTION SITE

Company:

Contact Person:

Phone Number:

Website:

E-mail:

VENDOR INFORMATION AT A GLANCE

CATERER

Company:

Contact Person:

Phone Number:

Website:

E-mail:

LIQUOR SERVICES

Company:

Contact Person:

Phone Number:

Website:

E-mail:

WEDDING GOWN

Company:

Contact Person:

Phone Number:

Website:

E-mail:

VENDOR INFORMATION AT A GLANCE

TUXEDO RENTAL

Company:

Contact Person:

Phone Number:

Website:

E-mail:

PHOTOGRAPHER

Company:

Contact Person:

Phone Number:

Website:

E-mail:

VIDEOGRAPHER

Company:

Contact Person:

Phone Number:

Website:

E-mail:

VENDOR INFORMATION AT A GLANCE

STATIONER

Company:

Contact Person:

Phone Number:

Website:

E-mail:

CALLIGRAPHER

Company:

Contact Person:

Phone Number:

Website:

E-mail:

MUSIC: CEREMONY

Company:

Contact Person:

Phone Number:

Website:

E-mail:

VENDOR INFORMATION AT A GLANCE

MUSIC: RECEPTION

Company:

Contact Person:

Phone Number:

Website:

E-mail:

FLORIST

Company:

Contact Person:

Phone Number:

Website:

E-mail:

BAKERY

Company:

Contact Person:

Phone Number:

Website:

E-mail:

VENDOR INFORMATION AT A GLANCE

DECORATIONS

Company:

Contact Person:

Phone Number:

Website:

E-mail:

ICE SCULPTURE

Company:

Contact Person:

Phone Number:

Website:

E-mail:

PARTY FAVORS

Company:

Contact Person:

Phone Number:

Website:

E-mail:

VENDOR INFORMATION AT A GLANCE

BALLOONIST

Company:

Contact Person:

Phone Number:

Website:

E-mail:

TRANSPORTATION

Company:

Contact Person:

Phone Number:

Website:

E-mail:

RENTAL & SUPPLIES:

Company:

Contact Person:

Phone Number:

Website:

E-mail:

VENDOR INFORMATION AT A GLANCE

GIFT SUPPLIERS

Company:

Contact Person:

Phone Number:

Website:

E-mail:

VALET SERVICES

Company:

Contact Person:

Phone Number:

Website:

E-mail:

GIFT ATTENDANT

Company:

Contact Person:

Phone Number:

Website:

E-mail:

VENDOR INFORMATION AT A GLANCE

REHEARSAL DINNER

Company:

Contact Person:

Phone Number:

Website:

E-mail:

OTHER:

Company:

Contact Person:

Phone Number:

Website:

E-mail:

OTHER:

Company:

Contact Person:

Phone Number:

Website:

E-mail:

WEDDING PLANNING CHECKLIST

- ❏ Announce your engagement.

- ❏ Select a date for your wedding.

- ❏ Hire a professional wedding consultant.

- ❏ Determine the type of wedding you want:
  location, formality, time of day, number of guests, etc.

- ❏ Determine a budget and how expenses will be shared.

- ❏ Develop a record-keeping system for payments made.

- ❏ Consolidate all guest lists: bride's, groom's,
  bride's family, groom's family, and organize
  as follows:
  - 1) those who must be invited
  - 2) those who should be invited
  - 3) those who would be nice to invite

- ❏ Decide if you want to include children among guests.

- ❏ Select and reserve a ceremony site.

- ❏ Select and reserve your officiant.

NINE MONTHS AND EARLIER (CONT'D)

- ❏ Select and reserve reception site.

- ❏ Select and order your bridal gown and headpiece.

- ❏ Determine your color scheme.

- ❏ Send engagement notice with a photograph to your local newspaper.

- ❏ Buy a calendar and note all important activities: showers, luncheons, parties, get-togethers, etc.

- ❏ If ceremony or reception is at home, arrange for home or garden improvements as needed.

- ❏ Select and book photographer.

- ❏ Order passport, visa, or birth certificate, if needed, for your honeymoon or marriage license.

- ❏ Select maid of honor, best man, bridesmaids, and ushers (approx. one usher per 50 guests).

WEDDING PLANNING CHECKLIST

SIX TO NINE MONTHS BEFORE WEDDING

- ❏ Select flower girl and ring bearer.
- ❏ Reserve wedding night bridal suite.
- ❏ Select attendants' dresses, shoes, and accessories.
- ❏ Select flower girl's dress, shoes, and accessories.
- ❏ Select and book caterer, if needed.
- ❏ Select and book ceremony musicians.
- ❏ Select and book reception musicians or DJ.
- ❏ Schedule fittings and delivery dates for yourself, attendants, flower girl, and ring bearer.
- ❏ Select and book videographer.
- ❏ Select and book florist.

FOUR TO SIX MONTHS BEFORE WEDDING

- ❏ Start shopping for each other's wedding gifts.
- ❏ Reserve rental items needed for ceremony/reception.
- ❏ Finalize guest list.
- ❏ Select and order invitations and other stationery items.
- ❏ Address invitations or hire a calligrapher.
- ❏ Set date, time, and location for your rehearsal dinner.
- ❏ Arrange accommodations for out-of-town guests.

WEDDING PLANNING CHECKLIST

FOUR TO SIX MONTHS BEFORE WEDDING (CONT'D)

- ❑ Start planning your honeymoon.
- ❑ Select and book all miscellaneous services, i.e. gift attendants, valet parking, etc.
- ❑ Purchase shoes and accessories.
- ❑ Begin to break-in your shoes.
- ❑ Register for wedding gifts.

TWO TO FOUR MONTHS BEFORE WEDDING

- ❑ Select bakery and order wedding cake.
- ❑ Order party favors.
- ❑ Select and order room decorations.
- ❑ Purchase honeymoon attire and luggage.
- ❑ Select and book wedding day transportation
- ❑ Check blood test and marriage license requirements.
- ❑ Shop for wedding rings and engrave them.
- ❑ Consider having your teeth cleaned or bleached.
- ❑ Consider writing a will and/or prenuptial agreement.
- ❑ Plan activities for out-of-town guests both before and after the wedding.
- ❑ Purchase gifts for wedding attendants.

WEDDING PLANNING CHECKLIST

SIX TO EIGHT WEEKS BEFORE WEDDING

- ❏ Mail invitations. Include accommodation choices and a map to assist guests in finding the ceremony and reception sites.

- ❏ Maintain a record of RSVPs and all gifts received. Send thank-you notes upon receipt of gifts.

- ❏ Determine hairstyle and makeup.

- ❏ Schedule to have your hair, makeup, and nails done the day of the wedding.

- ❏ Finalize shopping for wedding day accessories, such as toasting glasses, ring pillow, guest book, etc.

- ❏ Set up an area or a table in your home to display gifts as you receive them.

- ❏ Check with your local newspapers for wedding announcement requirements.

- ❏ Have your formal wedding portrait taken.

- ❏ Send wedding announcement and photograph to your local newspapers.

- ❏ Check requirements to change your name and address.

- ❏ Select and reserve wedding attire for groom, ushers, father of the bride, and ring bearer.

- ❏ Select a guest book attendant. Decide where and when to have guests sign in.

SIX TO EIGHT WEEKS BEFORE WEDDING (CONT'D)

- ❑ Mail invitations to rehearsal dinner.

- ❑ Get blood test and health certificate.

- ❑ Obtain marriage license.

- ❑ Plan a luncheon or dinner with your bridesmaids. Give them their gifts at that time or at the rehearsal dinner.

- ❑ Find "something old, something new, something borrowed, something blue, and a six pence (or shiny penny) for your shoe."

- ❑ Finalize your menu, beverage, and alcohol order.

- ❑ Review and update your gift registry.

WEDDING PLANNING CHECKLIST

TWO TO SIX WEEKS BEFORE WEDDING

- ❑ Confirm ceremony details with your officiant.

- ❑ Arrange final fitting of bridesmaids' dresses.

- ❑ Have final fitting of your gown and headpiece.

- ❑ Make final floral selections.

- ❑ Pick up rings and check for fit.

- ❑ Finalize rehearsal dinner plans; arrange seating and write names on place cards, if desired.

- ❑ Make a timeline for your wedding party.

- ❑ Make a detailed timeline for your service providers.

- ❑ Confirm details with all service providers, including attire. Give them a copy of your wedding timeline.

- ❑ Start packing for your honeymoon.

- ❑ Finalize addressing and stamping announcements.

- ❑ Decide if you want to form a receiving line. If so, determine when and where to form the line.

- ❑ Contact guests who haven't responded.

- ❑ Meet with photographer and confirm special photos you want.

- ❑ Meet with videographer and confirm special events or people you want videotaped.

WEDDING PLANNING CHECKLIST

TWO TO SIX WEEKS BEFORE WEDDING (CONT'D)

- ❏ Meet with musicians and confirm music to be played during special events, such as the first dance.

- ❏ Continue writing thank-you notes as gifts arrive.

- ❏ Remind bridesmaids and ushers of when and where to pick up their wedding attire.

- ❏ Purchase the lipstick, nail polish, and any other accessories you want your bridesmaids to wear.

- ❏ Determine ceremony seating for special guests. Give a list to the ushers.

- ❏ Plan reception room layout and seating with your reception site manager or caterer. Write names on place cards for arranged seating.

WEDDING PLANNING CHECKLIST

THE LAST WEEK

- ❑ Pick up wedding attire and make sure everything fits.

- ❑ Do final guest count and notify your caterer or reception site manager.

- ❑ Gather everything you will need for the rehearsal and wedding day.

- ❑ Arrange for someone to drive the getaway car.

- ❑ Review the schedule of events and last minute arrangements with your service providers. Give them each a detailed timeline.

- ❑ Confirm all honeymoon reservations and accommodations. Pick up tickets and travelers' checks.

- ❑ Finish packing your suitcases for the honeymoon.

- ❑ Familiarize yourself with guests' names. It will help during the receiving line and reception.

- ❑ Notify the post office to hold your mail while you are away on your honeymoon.

WEDDING PLANNING CHECKLIST

THE REHEARSAL DAY

- ❏ Review list of things to bring to the rehearsal.

- ❏ Put suitcases in getaway car.

- ❏ Give your bridesmaids the lipstick, nail polish, and accessories you want them to wear for the wedding.

- ❏ Give best man the officiant's fee and any other checks for service providers. Instruct him to deliver these checks the day of the wedding.

- ❏ Arrange for someone to bring accessories, such as flower basket, ring pillow, guest book and pen, toasting glasses, cake-cutting knife, and napkins to the ceremony and reception.

- ❏ Arrange for someone to mail announcements the day after the wedding.

- ❏ Arrange for someone to return rental items, such as tuxedos, slip, and cake pillars after the wedding.

- ❏ Provide each member of your wedding party with a detailed schedule of events/timelines for the wedding day.

- ❏ Review ceremony seating with ushers.

WEDDING PLANNING CHECKLIST

THE WEDDING DAY

- ❏ Review list of things to bring to the ceremony.

- ❏ Give the groom's ring to the maid of honor.

- ❏ Give the bride's ring to the best man.

- ❏ Simply follow your detailed schedule of events.

- ❏ Relax and enjoy your wedding!

CHECKLIST NOTES

CHECKLIST OF BUDGET ITEMS

CEREMONY

- ❏ Ceremony Site Fee
- ❏ *Officiant's Fee*
- ❏ *Officiant's Gratuity*
- ❏ Guest Book/Pen/Penholder
- ❏ Ring Bearer Pillow
- ❏ Flower Girl Basket

WEDDING ATTIRE

- ❏ Bridal Gown
- ❏ Alterations
- ❏ Headpiece & Veil
- ❏ Gloves
- ❏ Jewelry
- ❏ Stockings
- ❏ Garter
- ❏ Shoes
- ❏ Hairdresser
- ❏ Makeup Artist
- ❏ Manicure/Pedicure
- ❏ *Groom's Formal Wear*

Items in italics are traditionally paid for by the groom or his family.

CHECKLIST OF BUDGET ITEMS

PHOTOGRAPHY

- ❏ Bride & Groom's Album
- ❏ Parents' Album
- ❏ Extra Prints
- ❏ Proofs/Previews
- ❏ Negatives/Digital Files
- ❏ Engagement Photograph
- ❏ Formal Bridal Portrait

VIDEOGRAPHY

- ❏ Main Video
- ❏ Titles
- ❏ Extra Hours
- ❏ Photo Montage
- ❏ Extra Copies

STATIONERY

- ❏ Invitations
- ❏ Response Cards
- ❏ Reception Cards
- ❏ Ceremony Cards
- ❏ Pew Cards
- ❏ Seating/Place Cards
- ❏ Rain Cards/Maps
- ❏ Ceremony Programs
- ❏ Announcements
- ❏ Thank-You Notes
- ❏ Stamps
- ❏ Calligraphy
- ❏ Napkins/Matchbooks

Items in italics are traditionally paid for by the groom or his family.

CHECKLIST OF BUDGET ITEMS

RECEPTION

- ❏ Reception Site Fee
- ❏ Hors D' Oeuvres
- ❏ Main Meal/Caterer
- ❏ Liquor/Beverages
- ❏ Bartending Fee
- ❏ Bar Set-up Fee
- ❏ Corkage Fee
- ❏ Fee to Pour Coffee
- ❏ Service Providers' Meals
- ❏ Gratuity
- ❏ Party Favors
- ❏ Disposable Cameras
- ❏ Rose Petals/Rice
- ❏ Gift Attendant
- ❏ Parking Fee
- ❏ Valet Services

MUSIC

- ❏ Ceremony Music
- ❏ Reception Music

BAKERY

- ❏ Wedding Cake
- ❏ *Groom's Cake*
- ❏ Cake Delivery
- ❏ Set-Up Fee
- ❏ Cake-Cutting Fee
- ❏ Cake Top
- ❏ Cake Knife
- ❏ Toasting Glasses

Items in italics are traditionally paid for by the groom or his family.

CHECKLIST OF BUDGET ITEMS

FLOWERS

BOUQUETS
- ❏ *Bride*
- ❏ Tossing
- ❏ Maid of Honor
- ❏ Bridesmaids

FLORAL HAIRPIECES
- ❏ Maid of Honor
- ❏ Bridesmaids
- ❏ Flower Girls

CORSAGES
- ❏ *Bride's Going Away*
- ❏ *Other Family Members*

BOUTONNIERES
- ❏ *Groom*
- ❏ *Ushers*
- ❏ *Other Family Members*

CEREMONY SITE
- ❏ Main Altar
- ❏ Altar Candelabra
- ❏ Aisle Pew

RECEPTION SITE
- ❏ Reception Site
- ❏ Head Table
- ❏ Guest Tables
- ❏ Buffet Table
- ❏ Punch Table
- ❏ Cake Table
- ❏ Cake
- ❏ Cake Knife

Items in italics are traditionally paid for by the groom or his family.

WEDDING PLANNING CALENDAR

Month_____ 20_____ Number of months before wedding _____

Sunday	Monday	Tuesday	Wednesday	Thursday	Friday	Saturday

WEDDING PLANNING CALENDAR

Use the calendar on the following pages to document your wedding date, parties, all of your appointments, scheduled payments, and any other items you want to complete by a certain date.

If you are planning on a health, fitness, and/or beauty regime during your wedding planning process, write down your routine on this calendar to keep you on track and help you reach your goal.

How to use the calendar: Assign the last calendar page provided for the month your wedding will take place. Then work backwards and simply fill in the month, year, and number of months before your wedding at the top of each page. Then fill in the dates based on each month.

BUDGET NOTES

BUDGET ANALYSIS

	Budget	Actual
GIFTS (Typically = 3% of Budget)	$	$
Bride's, Groom's Gift	$	$
Bridesmaids', *Ushers' Gifts*	$	$
SUBTOTAL 13	$	$
PARTIES (Typically = 4% of Budget)	$	$
Bridesmaids' Luncheon	$	$
Rehearsal Dinner	$	$
SUBTOTAL 14	$	$
MISCELLANEOUS (Typically = 4% of Budget)	$	$
Newspaper Announcements	$	$
Marriage License	$	$
Prenuptial Agreement	$	$
Bridal Gown/Bouquet Preservation	$	$
Wedding Consultant	$	$
Wedding Planning Software	$	$
Taxes	$	$
SUBTOTAL 15	$	$
GRAND TOTAL	$	$
(Add "Budget" & "Actual" Subtotals 1-15)		

Items in italics are traditionally paid for by the groom or his family.

BUDGET ANALYSIS

	Budget	Actual
Toasting Glasses	$	$
Floral Delivery/Set-up	$	$
SUBTOTAL 9	$	$
DECORATIONS (Typically = 3% of Budget)	$	$
Table Centerpieces	$	$
Balloons	$	$
SUBTOTAL 10	$	$
TRANSPORTATION (Typically = 2% of Budget)	$	$
Transportation	$	$
SUBTOTAL 11	$	$
RENTAL ITEMS (Typically = 3% of Budget)	$	$
Bridal Slip	$	$
Ceremony Accessories	$	$
Tent/Canopy	$	$
Dance Floor	$	$
Tables/Chairs	$	$
Linen/Tableware	$	$
Heaters, Lanterns	$	$
SUBTOTAL 12	$	$

Items in italics are traditionally paid for by the groom or his family.

	Budget	Actual
Tossing	$	$
Maid of Honor	$	$
Bridesmaids	$	$
FLORAL HAIRPIECES		
Maid of Honor	$	$
Bridesmaids	$	$
Flower Girl	$	$
CORSAGES		
Bride's Going Away	$	$
Other Family Members	$	$
BOUTONNIERES		
Groom	$	$
Ushers, Other Family Members	$	$
CEREMONY SITE FLOWERS		
Main Altar	$	$
Altar Candelabra	$	$
Aisle Pews	$	$
RECEPTION SITE FLOWERS		
Reception Site	$	$
Head Table	$	$
Guest Tables	$	$
Buffet Table	$	$
Punch Table	$	$
Cake Table	$	$
Cake	$	$
Cake Knife	$	$

Items in italics are traditionally paid for by the groom or his family.

BUDGET ANALYSIS

	Budget	Actual
Gratuity	$	$
Party Favors, Disposable Cameras	$	$
Rose Petals/Rice	$	$
Gift Attendant	$	$
Parking Fee, Valet Services	$	$
SUBTOTAL 6	$	$
MUSIC (Typically = 5% of Budget)	$	$
Ceremony Music	$	$
Reception Music	$	$
SUBTOTAL 7	$	$
BAKERY (Typically = 2% of Budget)	$	$
Wedding Cake	$	$
Groom's Cake	$	$
Cake Delivery, Set-Up Fee	$	$
Cake-Cutting Fee	$	$
Cake Top, Cake Knife, Toasting Glasses	$	$
SUBTOTAL 8	$	$
FLOWERS (Typically = 6% of Budget)	$	$
BOUQUETS		
Bride	$	$

Items in italics are traditionally paid for by the groom or his family.

BUDGET ANALYSIS

	Budget	Actual
STATIONERY (Typically = 4% of Budget)	$	$
Invitations	$	$
Response Cards	$	$
Reception Cards	$	$
Ceremony Cards	$	$
Pew Cards	$	$
Seating/Place Cards	$	$
Rain Cards/Maps	$	$
Ceremony Programs	$	$
Announcements	$	$
Thank-You Notes	$	$
Stamps	$	$
Calligraphy	$	$
Napkins/Matchbooks	$	$
SUBTOTAL 5	$	$
RECEPTION (Typically = 35% of Budget)	$	$
Reception Site Fee	$	$
Hors D' Oeuvres	$	$
Main Meal/Caterer	$	$
Liquor/Beverages	$	$
Bartending Fee, Bar Set-up Fee	$	$
Corkage Fee	$	$
Fee To Pour Coffee	$	$
Service Providers' Meals	$	$

Items in italics are traditionally paid for by the groom or his family.

BUDGET ANALYSIS

	Budget	Actual
Hairdresser	$	$
Makeup Artist	$	$
Manicure/Pedicure	$	$
Groom's Formal Wear	$	$
SUBTOTAL 2	$	$
PHOTOGRAPHY (Typically = 9% of Budget)	$	$
Bride & Groom's Album	$	$
Parents' Album	$	$
Extra Prints	$	$
Proofs/Previews	$	$
Negatives/Digital Files	$	$
Engagement Photograph	$	$
Formal Bridal Portrait	$	$
SUBTOTAL 3	$	$
VIDEOGRAPHY (Typically = 5% of Budget)	$	$
Main Video	$	$
Titles	$	$
Extra Hours	$	$
Photo Montage	$	$
Extra Copies	$	$
SUBTOTAL 4	$	$

Items in italics are traditionally paid for by the groom or his family.

BUDGET ANALYSIS

WEDDING BUDGET	Budget	Actual
YOUR TOTAL WEDDING BUDGET	$	$
CEREMONY (Typically = 5% of Budget)	$	$
Ceremony Site Fee	$	$
Officiant's Fee	$	$
Officiant's Gratuity	$	$
Guest Book/Pen/Penholder	$	$
Ring Bearer Pillow	$	$
Flower Girl Basket	$	$
SUBTOTAL 1	$	$
WEDDING ATTIRE (Typically = 10% of Budget)	$	$
Bridal Gown	$	$
Alterations	$	$
Headpiece & Veil	$	$
Gloves	$	$
Jewelry	$	$
Stockings	$	$
Garter	$	$
Shoes	$	$

Items in italics are traditionally paid for by the groom or his family.

CHECKLIST OF BUDGET ITEMS

PARTIES

- ❏ Bridesmaids' Luncheon
- ❏ *Rehearsal Dinner*

MISCELLANEOUS

- ❏ Newspaper Announcement
- ❏ *Marriage License*
- ❏ *Prenuptial Agreement*
- ❏ Bridal Gown/Bouquet Preservation
- ❏ Wedding Consultant
- ❏ Wedding Planning Software
- ❏ Taxes

Items in italics are traditionally paid for by the groom or his family.

CHECKLIST OF BUDGET ITEMS

FLOWERS (CONT'D)

- ❏ Toasting Glasses
- ❏ Floral Delivery/Set-up

DECORATIONS

- ❏ Table Centerpieces
- ❏ Balloons

TRANSPORTATION

- ❏ Transportation

RENTAL ITEMS

- ❏ Bridal Slip
- ❏ Ceremony Accessories
- ❏ Tent/Canopy
- ❏ Dance Floor
- ❏ Tables/Chairs
- ❏ Linen/Tableware
- ❏ Heaters
- ❏ Lanterns

GIFTS

- ❏ *Bride's Gift*
- ❏ Groom's Gift
- ❏ Bridesmaids' Gifts
- ❏ *Ushers' Gifts*

Items in italics are traditionally paid for by the groom or his family.

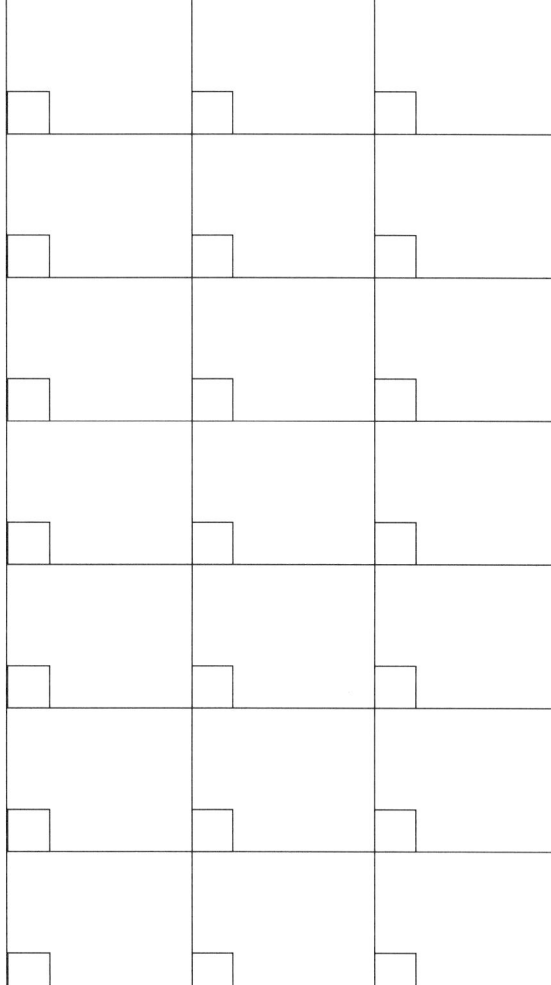

Month_____ 20_____ Number of months before wedding _____

Sunday	Monday	Tuesday	Wednesday	Thursday	Friday	Saturday

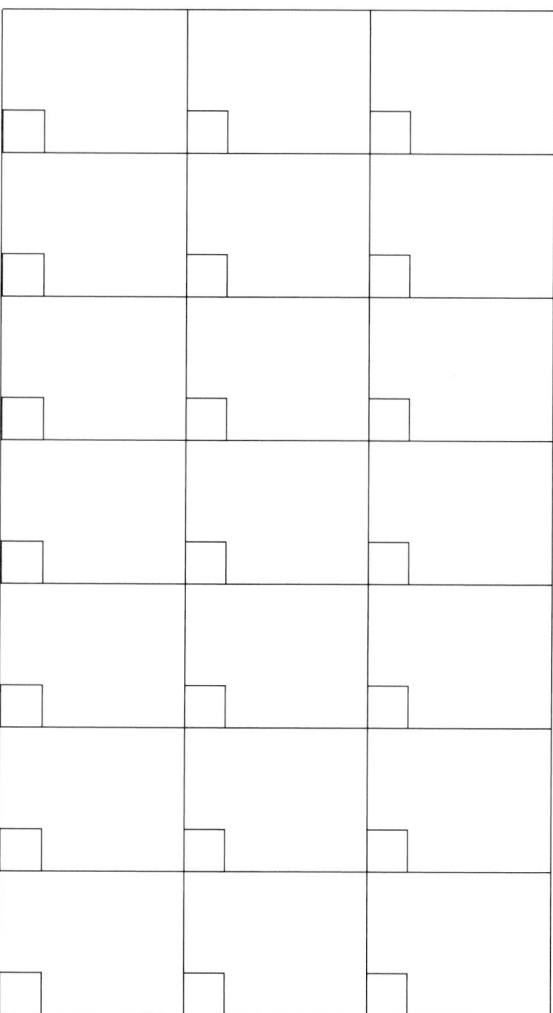

WEDDING PLANNING CALENDAR

Month_____   20_____   Number of months before wedding _____

Sunday	Monday	Tuesday	Wednesday	Thursday	Friday	Saturday

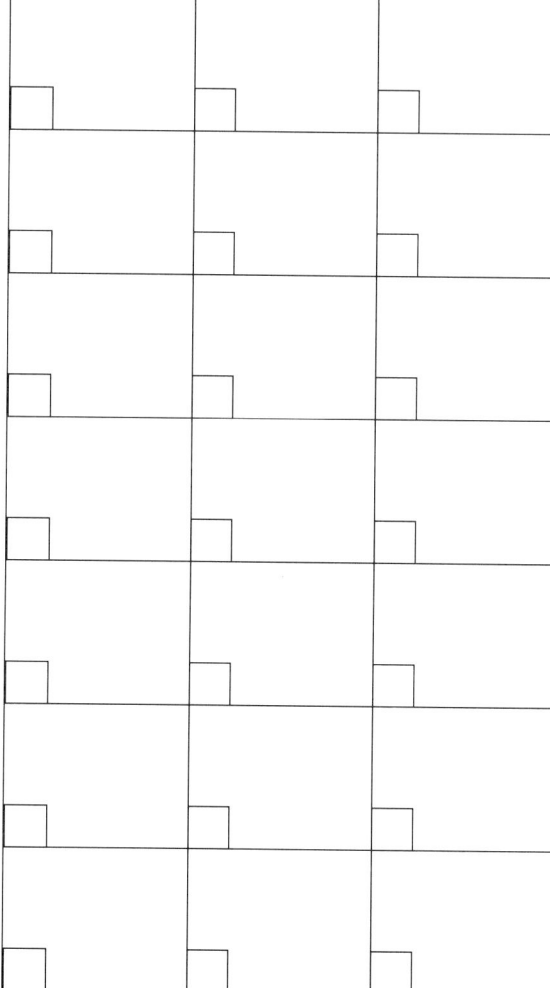

WEDDING PLANNING CALENDAR

Month_____ 20_____ Number of months before wedding _____

Sunday	Monday	Tuesday	Wednesday	Thursday	Friday	Saturday

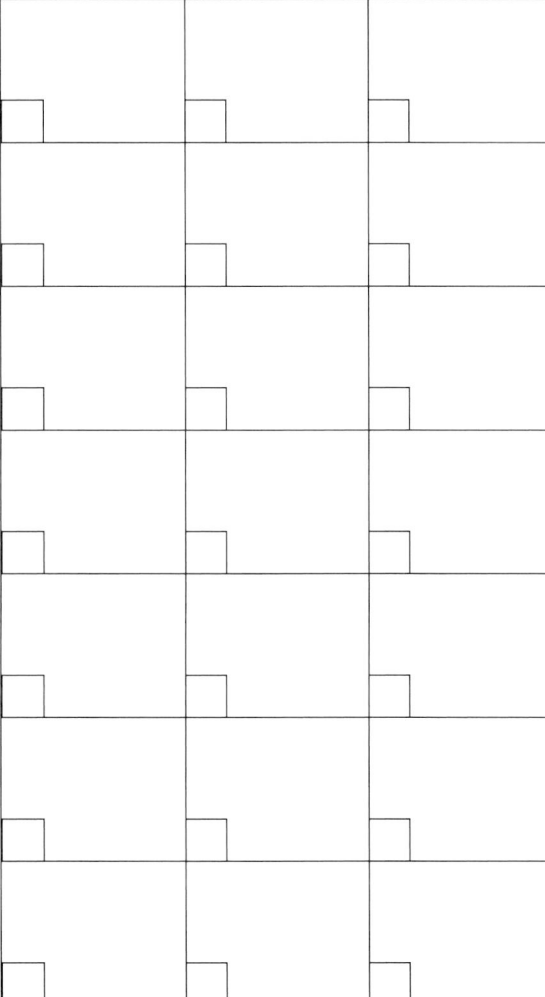

WEDDING PLANNING CALENDAR

Month_____ 20_____ Number of months before wedding _____

Sunday	Monday	Tuesday	Wednesday	Thursday	Friday	Saturday

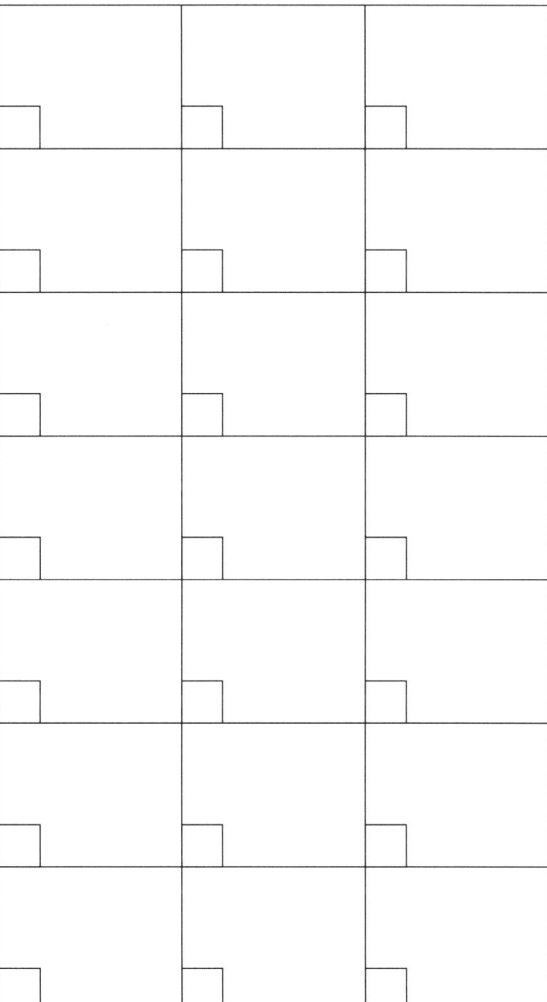

Month_____   20_____   Number of months before wedding _____

Sunday	Monday	Tuesday	Wednesday	Thursday	Friday	Saturday

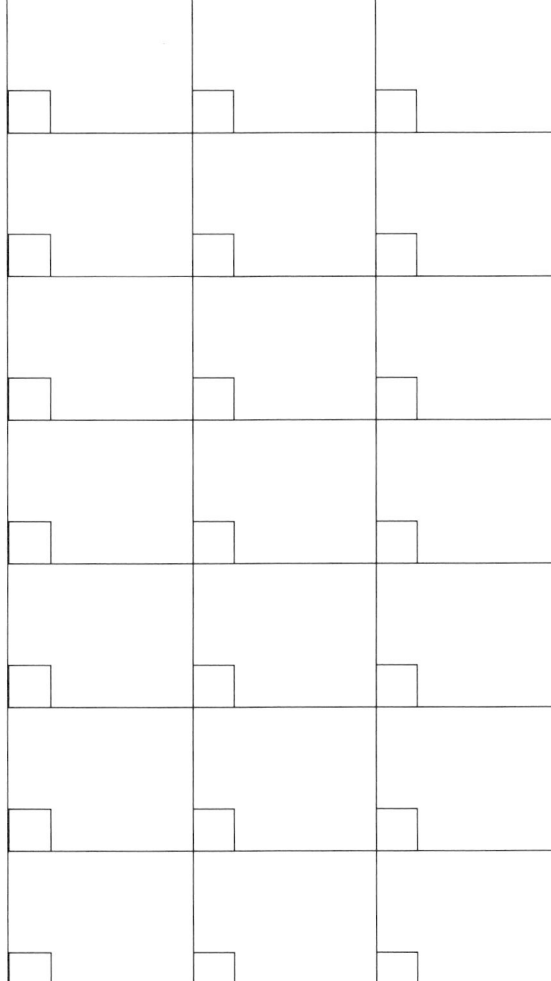

WEDDING PLANNING CALENDAR

Month_____ 20_____ Number of months before wedding _____

Sunday	Monday	Tuesday	Wednesday	Thursday	Friday	Saturday

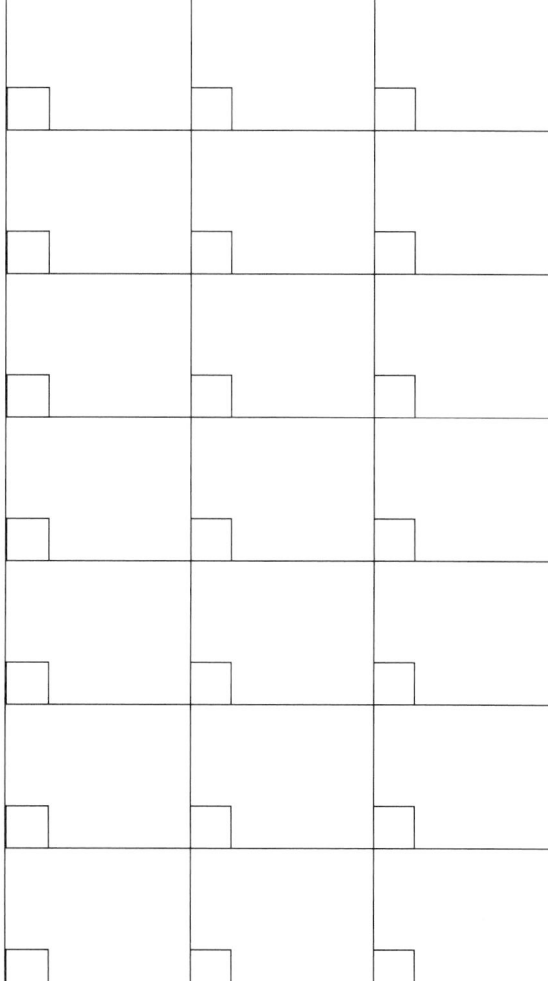

WEDDING PLANNING CALENDAR

Month_____ 20_____ Number of months before wedding _____

Sunday	Monday	Tuesday	Wednesday	Thursday	Friday	Saturday

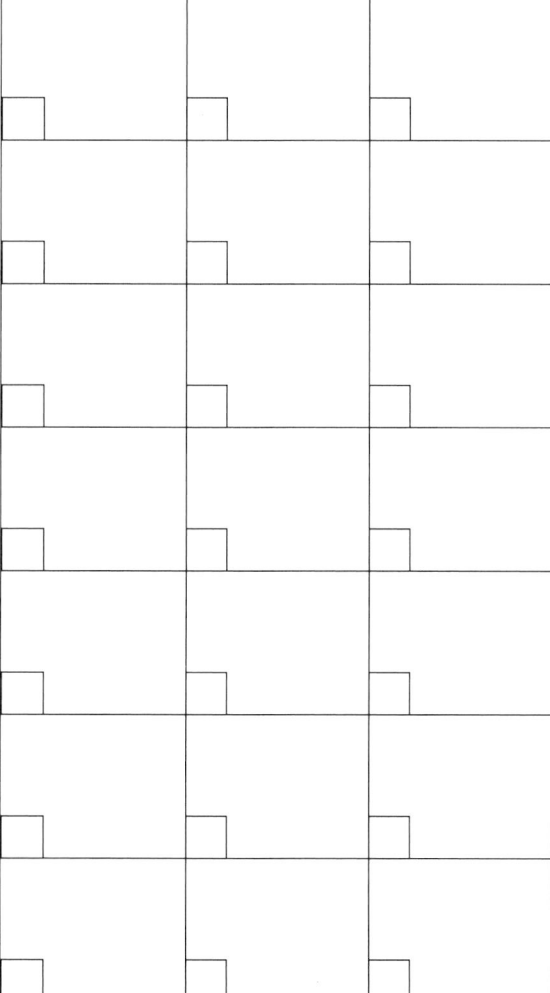

Month_____ 20_____ Number of months before wedding _____

Sunday	Monday	Tuesday	Wednesday	Thursday	Friday	Saturday

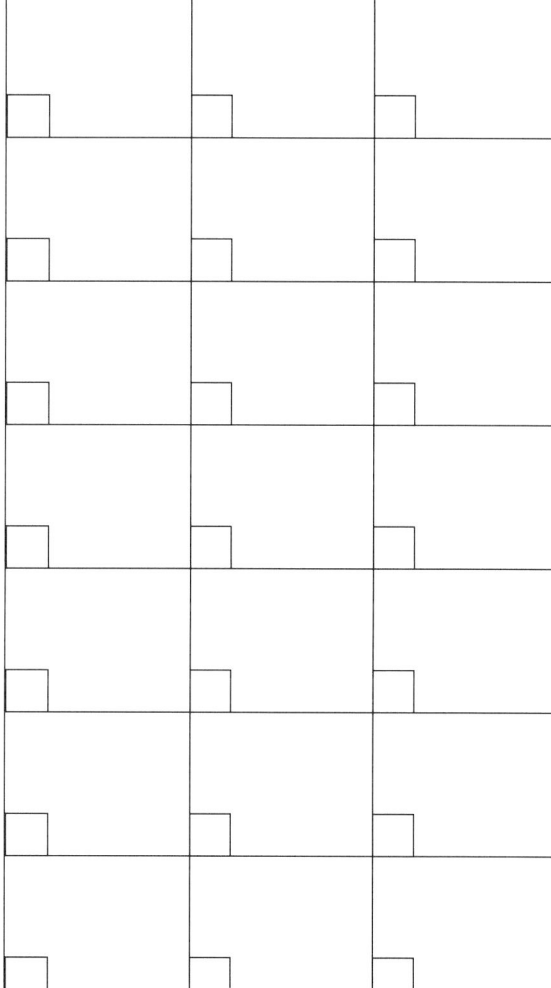

WEDDING PLANNING CALENDAR

Month_____   20_____   Number of months before wedding _____

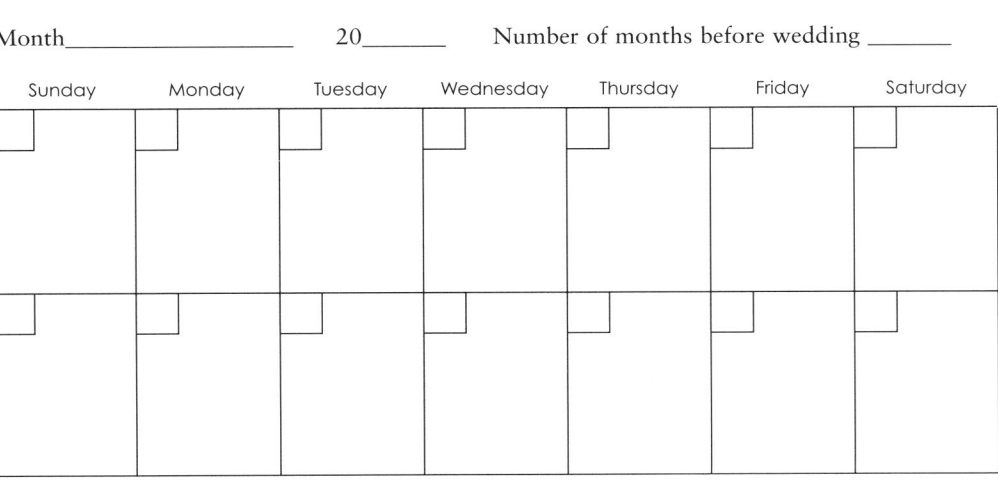

Sunday	Monday	Tuesday	Wednesday	Thursday	Friday	Saturday

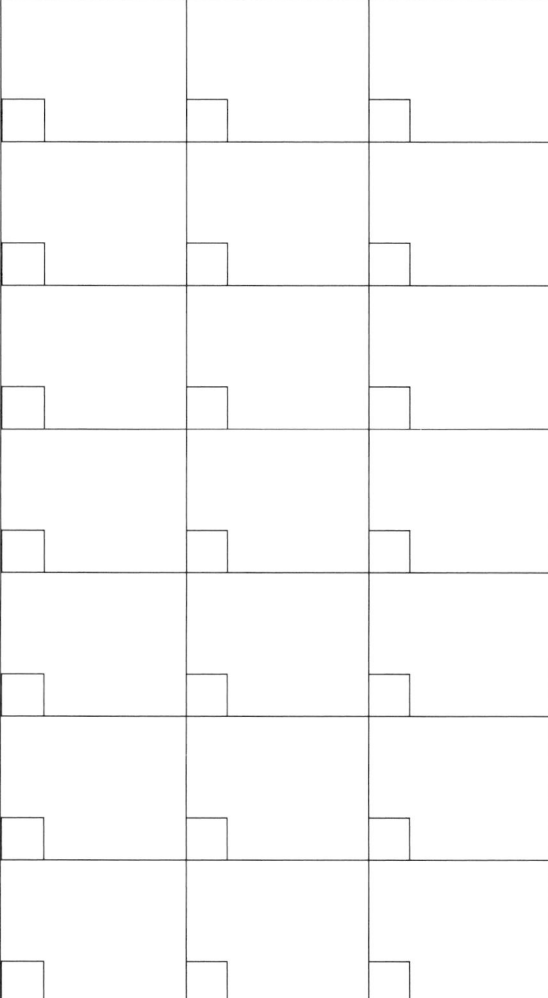

Month_____ 20_____ Number of months before wedding _____

Sunday	Monday	Tuesday	Wednesday	Thursday	Friday	Saturday

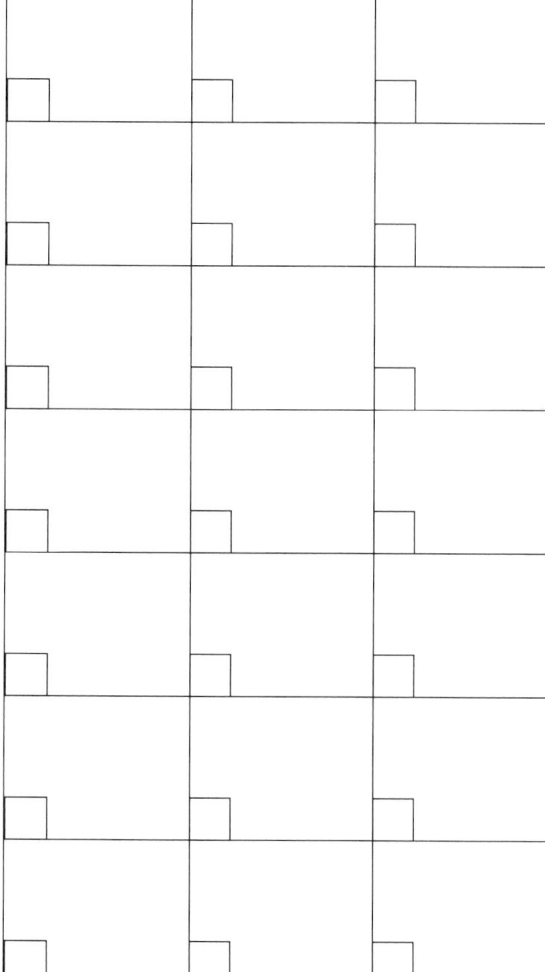

Month_____ 20_____ Number of months before wedding _____

Sunday	Monday	Tuesday	Wednesday	Thursday	Friday	Saturday

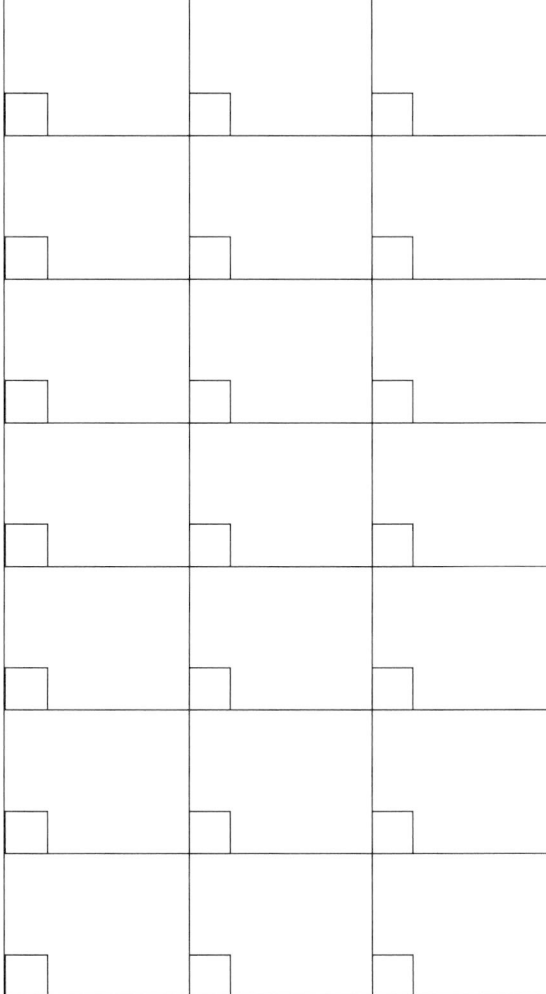

WEDDING PLANNING NOTES

WEDDING PLANNING NOTES

WEDDING PLANNING NOTES